DEFENDING THE EARTH

Abuses of Human Rights and the Environment

June 1992

Human Rights Watch
Natural Resources Defense Council

Printed in the United States of America
Printed on recycled paper
Cover design by Deborah Thomas

Library of Congress Catalog Card No. 92-72323
ISBN 1-56432-073-1

HUMAN RIGHTS WATCH

Human Rights Watch, which monitors and promotes observance of internationally recognized human rights worldwide, is composed of Africa Watch, Americas Watch, Asia Watch, Helsinki Watch, Middle East Watch, and the Fund for Free Expression.

NATURAL RESOURCES DEFENSE COUNCIL

The Natural Resources Defense Council is a nonprofit membership organization dedicated to protecting the planet's natural resources and to improving the quality of the human environment. With 170,000 members and a staff of lawyers, scientists, and environmental specialists, NRDC combines the power of law, the power of science, and the power of people in defense of the environment.

CONTENTS

ACKNOWLEDGMENTS i
PREFACE iii
INTRODUCTION v
BRAZIL: Rural Violence and the Rainforest 1
ERITREA: A War on the Environment 11
INDIA: Before the Deluge 21
KENYA: Environmental Heroine or 'Traitor'? 39
MALAYSIA: An Unholy Alliance 45
MEXICO: Cutting Through the Haze 65
PHILIPPINES: A Dangerous Environment for Activists 77
THE FORMER SOVIET UNION: A Poisonous Legacy 89
UNITED STATES: Punishing Whistleblowers 97

ACKNOWLEDGMENTS

Staff, consultants and volunteers for Human Rights Watch and the Natural Resources Defense Council contributed to this report. The authors of case studies from Human Rights Watch are Alex DeWaal (Eritrea), Patricia Gossman (India), Lydia Lobenthal (Malaysia), Jemera Rone and Dan Swanson (Brazil), and Julie Triedman (Philippines). The authors of case studies from NRDC are Lynn Fischer and Christine MacDonald (Mexico), David O'Very (United States of America), Crystal Straube (Kenya), and Kristen Suokko (former Soviet Union). Gara LaMarche and S. Jacob Scherr edited the report. We also acknowledge assistance from Lisa Fleischman and Baylor Semple; Elizabeth Barratt-Brown, David Christensen, and Glenn Prickett from NRDC; and numerous other individuals and organizations worldwide who helped in providing information and suggestions for this report.

Finally, we deeply appreciate the generous support of the Nathan S. Cummings Foundation, which made this report possible.

PREFACE

This report is the result of an unprecedented joint effort between two leading citizen advocacy organizations: a human rights group, Human Rights Watch; and an environmental group, the Natural Resources Defense Council. As one who has been for 14 years privileged to be involved with both, I have long believed that a cooperative effort such as this one will enhance both causes significantly.

Abuses of human rights often exist in tandem with environmental degradation. Suppression of dissent -- often violent -- is frequently employed by governments to silence opposition to harmful political and social policies and development schemes that could not withstand public scrutiny, and to forestall public concern about environmental decay. The case studies in this report demonstrate a linkage between human rights and environmental abuses that is global in scope, occurring in both industrialized and developing countries.

Issuing this joint report at the time of the Earth Summit in Rio de Janeiro will focus attention on the relationship, often causal, between human rights and environmental abuses. We also hope that it marks the start of future exchanges between the two groups of advocates, so that both causes will benefit from an expanded constituency for their concerns.

Adrian W. DeWind
Chair, Natural Resources Defense Council
Vice Chair, Human Rights Watch

INTRODUCTION

Shortly after assuming the Presidency of Czechoslovakia in 1990, Vaclav Havel told the nation's people: "We have laid waste to our soil and the rivers and forests that our forefathers bequeathed to us, and we have the worst environment in the whole of Europe today." What President Havel did not mention -- and did not have to -- is that Czechoslovakia's natural environment could be poisoned with impunity because of the previous regime's near-total control of citizen organizations, the press, universities and other potential sources of oversight and criticism.

Today, Czechoslovakia has the chance, with the restoration of a free press, an unfettered academy, a reformed bar and judiciary and other essential elements of civil society, to redress the environmental degradation made possible by the suppression of government information and public concern about the environment. In all too many other countries around the world, human rights abuses continue to shield environmental abuses -- and block meaningful and effective efforts to deal with them.

Repressive governments often defend their practices by asserting that human rights -- particularly freedoms of expression, association, and participation in decisionmaking -- are esoteric, and must take a back seat to the need to preserve order or foster economic development. We believe otherwise. All over the world, people die and suffer from environmental calamities and degradation that could have been avoided if the policies and practices that led to them had been subjected to public scrutiny and debate.

A striking example of this is China's callous disregard for the environment as part of its campaign of suppression in Tibet, where it plans a massive power station at Yamdrok Tso, a lake which has religious significance and is also a key source of sustenance for local residents. Even in a relatively open society as the United States of America, there is concern that hazardous facilities are disproportionately located in less politically powerful communities inhabited by minorities and the poor. In the conclusion of a recent Panos Institute study of the impact of apartheid on the environment of South Africa, Dr. Mamphela Ramphele wrote that "participatory democracy is a vital prerequisite for the upgrading of the environment, enabling people to reclaim control and to hold authorities accountable for the communities they purport to serve."[1]

This is clearly a matter of global concern. The secrecy that permitted the former Soviet Union to pollute the environment has had an impact beyond its own borders -- in Norway, for example, in a noxious nickel smelting plant that emits more sulfur dioxide than any Norwegian source, and in unsafe reindeer meat contaminated by Chernobyl.[2] The ability of the international community to address global environmental problems, such as climate change and biological impoverishment, will depend ultimately upon the empowerment of concerned citizens in every country to assure that national governments fulfill their international commitments.

A REPORT FOR THE EARTH SUMMIT

In June 1992, some 100 national leaders will gather in Rio de Janeiro for the United Nations Conference on Environment and Development, dubbed the "Earth Summit". Among the documents before them for adoption will be the draft Rio Declaration, a statement of principles on general rights and obligations. Principle 10 of the draft Declaration links human rights and environmental imperatives. It states that:

> At the national level, each individual shall have appropriate access to information concerning the environment that is held by public authorities, including information on hazardous materials and activities in their communities, and the opportunity to participate in decision-making processes. States shall facilitate and encourage public awareness and participation by making information widely available. Effective access to judicial and

---

[1] Panos Institute, *Restoring the Land: Environment and Change in Post-Apartheid South Africa*, (Mamphela Ramphele, ed., London: 1991), p. 202.

[2] "On Norway's Border, Russian Arctic in Crisis", *New York Times*, May 10, 1992, p. A1.

administrative proceedings, including redress and remedy, shall be provided.[3]

This report documents in various countries the governmental harassment of individuals and groups working to protect the environment and governmental suppression of environmental debate. We want to demonstrate that the protection of the environmental rights in Principle 10 of the draft Rio Declaration are prerequisite for meaningful efforts to deal with environmental degradation -- or, for that matter, with other social problem facing the world today.

The draft Rio Declaration does state in Principle 1 that "[Human beings] are entitled to a healthy and productive life in harmony with nature." Similar expressions of a right to a healthy environment can be found in other international and national normative statements, and the U.N. Sub-Commission on Human Rights now has a comprehensive study underway on the relationship between human rights and the environment. However, it is not our intent here to address the issues of whether there exists a substantive human right to a safe, sustainable environment or whether nature itself has rights which must be protected.[4]

---

[3] Preparatory Committee for the United Nations Conference on Environment and Development, Fourth Session, *Rio Declaration on Environment and Development*, A/CONF. 151/PC/WG. III/L.33/Rev.1, New York, April 2, 1992.

[4] For a recent discussion of these issues and of environmental "due process" rights, see the report of the Conference on "Earth Rights and Responsibilities: Human Rights and Environmental Protection," Yale Law School, April 3-5, 1992. The papers presented at the conference are to be published in a forthcoming special issue of the *Yale Journal of International Law*. Copies of the Earth Rights Conference report are available from NRDC.

WHO IS AN ENVIRONMENTALIST?

In preparing this report, we have chosen to emphasize the nature of a dispute or controversy as an environmental *issue* rather than the nature of group or individual being harassed as an environmental *advocate*. In today's world, there are many "environmentalists:" scientists, teachers, labor organizers, church leaders, indigenous peoples, elected officials, and women and men of all walks of life who express their concerns about threats to their health and welfare from environmental pollution or degradation -- such as air and water pollution, toxic waste dumping, deforestation, and displacement through massive development projects. In other words, environmentalists are people everywhere who are concerned about the safety and soundness of the natural systems upon which they and ultimately life on this planet depend.

METHODS FOR SUPPRESSING ENVIRONMENTAL DISCUSSION AND DEBATE

This report contains nine case studies on the overlap between human rights and environmental concerns. We include an account of the environmental legacy of the extreme repression which characterized the former Soviet Union. At the other end of the spectrum, we consider democratic societies like contemporary India, which has engaged in police abuses and used its "Official Secrets Act" to suppress opposition to an environmentally hazardous dam project. The remaining case studies feature a mix of regions, political systems and environmental problems:

- **Brazil,** where rural activists fighting the destruction of the rain forest have been murdered;

- **Eritrea**, where war has led to a ravaging of the natural environment, and the government has disguised its role in fostering drought by withholding rainfall records from the public;

- **Kenya**, where the opponent of a massive high-rise office tower that would have destroyed a park in Nairobi has been denounced and harassed as a "traitor" by the repressive Moi regime;

- **Malaysia**, where repressive internal security laws have been used to detain and harass anti-logging activists;

- **Mexico**, where the government has tried to co-opt environmental activists and conceal information about environmental hazards;

- **Philippines**, where criminal libel laws have been used to deter the press from exposing environmental abuses;

- **United States**, where "whistleblowers" who alert the public to safety hazards in the nuclear weapons industry have been persecuted, demoted and fired.

As these case studies demonstrate, governments use a variety of means to suppress environmental debates, including:

SUPPRESSION OF ENVIRONMENTAL CAMPAIGNERS

Physical attacks. Many people are familiar with the Chico Mendes case in Brazil. But since his murder, his successors as leaders of the trade unionists in Acre have received death threats, and some have gone into hiding. Among them are Mendes' widow, Ilzamar, his brother Jose Alves Mendes Neto, Gomercindo Clovis Rodrigues, Raimundo de Barros, Julio Barbosa de Aquino, Francisco de Assis Monteiro de Oliveira, and Mendes' successor as head of the Rubber Tappers Union, Osmarino Amancio Rodrigues. They are reportedly on a death list of 25 people drawn up by local landowners. The authorities have done little to provide protection or investigate the circumstances.

In the Philippines in October 1991, Father Nery Lito Satur was murdered by three armed men believed to be connected to illegal loggers on the island of Mindanao. Fr. Satur was heavily involved with a local campaign against illegal logging and had recently helped government officials in a series of arrests and confiscations of logs and equipment. Henry Domoldol, an Isnog tribal leader, was murdered by suspected paramilitary in July 1991 after a series of death threats. He had been a leader in the effort to protect the remaining stands of rainforest upon which the tribe depends. Members of the environmental group Haribon were arrested and accused of subversion by the local military when they exposed illegal logging of protected ebony trees on Palawan, in spite of the fact that they were cooperating with the Department of Environment. The local military is reportedly involved in the lucrative trade.

Imprisonment. The deforestation of southern Thailand has brought on mud slides that have killed hundreds of villagers. Buddhist monk Phra Prachak Kuttacitto, who works to protect the Dong Yai forest from illegal logging, has been arrested at least twice on charges of inciting unrest.[5]

Denunciation and harassment. Human rights and environmental groups have called attention to the political and police harassment of Kenyan Professor Wangari Mathaai, president of the Green Belt environmental group, who has been an outspoken critic of President Daniel Arap Moi's autocratic rule. Mathaai is famous for designing a community-oriented tree planting project that fought Kenyan deforestation. When she campaigned against President Moi's plan to destroy a park in order to build a 60-story high rise in downtown Nairobi, he labelled her an enemy of the government.

Libel suits. Libel suits are another common tactic for stifling environmental criticism. In the Philippines -- which still retains criminal libel laws which can result in the imprisonment of reporters -- logger Jose Alvarez sued the *Far Eastern Economic Review* over an article discussing his links to political and military leaders involved in the 1988 murders of Antonio Pimpas, a town councilor in Palawan, who was shot hours after stopping a truck full of logs, and Augusan del Sur, who was killed shortly after filing a complaint with the Department of Labor on behalf of workers at a local logging company seeking back wages, overtime and vacation pay.

In the United States, environmental groups are being "SLAPPed" for exercising their constitutional right of petition. These suits, which take their name from the acronym for "Strategic Lawsuits Against Public Participation," are being brought by corporations, real estate developers, government officials, and others against those who oppose them on issues of public concern. SLAPP targets have been sued for writing a letter to the editor, calling a public official, conducting a public campaign, speaking at a town meeting, testifying before Congress or state legislatures, and filing a public-interest lawsuit -- all activities at the core of advocacy protected by the First Amendment. SLAPP suits have been

---

[5] "Thai Soldiers Head Drunken Charge Against Buddhist Monastery," *Reuters*, September 10, 1991.

filed against two Missouri women who wrote letters to the editor criticizing the operation of an infectious waste incinerator; the American Academy of Pediatrics, sued by Alta Dena Dairy for $220 million after testimony before Congress about dangers of raw "certified" milk; and Plan-Kent, a citizens' group in the town of Kent in rural Putnam County, the site of reservoirs serving New York City, for opposing a proposed development of attached town houses on the grounds that no study had been done to assess its environmental impact.[6]

RESTRICTIONS ON ASSOCIATION AND ASSEMBLY

Many governments have excessive powers to regulate -- and therefore control -- private non-governmental organizations. In Indonesia, the site of tension between the military and activists for both the environment and human rights, local political and religious organizations which champion these two causes have been pressured to disband on the basis of a 1985 law regulating mass organizations. One of the groups in question, The Study Group For The Development of People's Initiative (abbreviated KSPPM in Indonesian) provides legal aid to villagers in North Tapanuli whose land and livelihood was threatened by a pulp factory called Indorayon. Indigenous Sumatran residents protested the development of the factory because they feared expropriation of the land by the company; there would be deforestation in some areas coupled with the supplanting of grazing lands with eucalyptus trees which would disrupt the local irrigation system; and the plant would produce industrial waste pollution.[7]

When groups require a government imprimatur in order to operate, delay can also be an effective tactic -- Malaysian environmentalists seeking to organize in the early 1970's faced a six-month wait from the Registrar of Societies.

---

[6]See "SLAPPing Down Critics," *The Fund for Free Expression*, July 1991.

[7]"Indonesia: Attempts to Intimidate Labor and Environmental Activists in North Sumatra," *News from Asia Watch*, April 15, 1992.

MISTREATMENT OF "WHISTLEBLOWERS"

Firing or punishing government "whistleblowers" is another tactic used by governments to silence those who question misguided environmental policies and expose official misconduct.

In 1988, the government of Benin struck a secret deal with a British corporation that would have given it the right to dump 50 million tons of chemical waste in the south of the country over a period of ten years. Despite the company's initial denials, it was determined that most of the waste would have been toxic. When Benin's health minister, Andre Atchade, protested the plans in a confidential memo, he was put under house arrest.[8] In Mexico, scientists who questioned the government's nuclear power plans were fired from their positions at the Federal Electricity Commission.[9]

In the United States, John Mumma was forcibly reassigned from his position as Northern Regional Forester for the U.S. Forest Service for refusing to yield to political pressure to permit more timber-cutting in Montan and northern Idaho in violation of environmental laws. Lorraine Mintzmyer, Rocky Mountain regional director for the National Park Service, was transferred after she raised questions about a controversial "vision report" that would have stepped up development of Yellowstone National Park.[10]

RESTRICTIONS ON THE MEDIA

Because the press plays a critical role in stimulating public awareness and sustaining public discussion of environmental issues, the media and journalists are often the target of officials and others eager to suppress debate of controversial matters.

---

[8] "African Wasteland," *Index on Censorship*, June/July 1989, p. 34.

[9] "Nuclear Debaters Fired in Mexico," *Index on Censorship*, June/July 1989.

[10] *High Country News*, October 7, 1991, p. 7.

Censorship. Chinese journalist Dai Qing incurred the wrath of Premier Li Peng by opposing the Three Gorges Dam project, which would have flooded the Yangtze River and displaced over a million people. In early 1989, she defied a ban on public discussion of the project by publishing a book of articles on the subject. After the crackdown following Tiananmen Square, she was arrested, and the remaining copies of her book were seized and burned, on the grounds that it was published "with the intention of preparing public opinion for turmoil."[11]

Japan's International Cooperation Agency excised from a training film about development and the environment sections of the film's narrative commentary such as "a tropical rain forest, once destroyed, can rarely be restored to its original state."[12]

Physical attacks on journalists. In May 1989, journalist Barbara D'Achille, Peru's leading writer on ecology and the environment, was stoned to death by Shining Path guerrillas, along with Esteban Bohorquez, an expert on llamas. D'Achille, a staunch defender of conservation projects, had written frequently on the environmental effects of coca cultivation, which include deforestation, chemical pollution, and erosion, especially in the Upper Huallaga River Valley.[13]

RESTRICTIONS ON ACCESS TO INFORMATION HELD BY GOVERNMENT

Governments know that "information is power" and have taken steps to conceal information about environmental issues so as to undercut public concerns and the ability of the public to respond.

In India, environmentalists have gone to their Supreme Court on claims that their government is covering up the seriousness of air

---

[11] Interview with Dai Qing in *Human Rights Tribune*, Spring 1992.

[12] "The Case of the Disappearing Shrimp," *Index on Censorship*, July 1991, p. 17.

[13] "Peruvian Guerrillas Slay Journalist," *Chicago Tribune*, June 2, 1989, p. C20.

pollution threats to the Taj Mahal.[14] In 1989, the India state of Gujarat implemented plans to build dams along the Narmada River, beginning the displacement of over 1.5 million indigenous tribal peasants and farmers. Citing India's Official Secrets Act, the government imposed a news blackout on twelve affected villages along the Narmada River. When 8,000 activists and residents protested, 5,000 were arrested. After intense pressure, the news blackout was lifted, but the dam project continues. Contrast this with the fate of a similar project in Botswana, scuttled after the government -- which has what may well be the strongest record on freedom of expression of any African country -- invited public comment about its plans.

Former governments in Ethiopia kept official rainfall records secret, because it served their interests to falsely claim that drought was the cause of persistent famine -- where in reality, army activities and agricultural policies were more often to blame. In 1989, Moroccan authorities withheld from the public for ten days the news of a major oil spill off the Atlantic coast.

In the United States, Physicians for Social Responsibility has accused the Energy Department of improperly invoking national security to shield access to data about the health effects of low level radiation.[15]

LOOKING TO THE FUTURE

In our view, the strongest premise for cooperation between human rights and environmental organizations is the recognition that the two communities have distinctly different, yet interdependent, mandates. We agree with human rights advocate Kerry Kennedy Cuomo, who recently investigated abuses of human rights and the environment on the island of Palawan in the Philippines, that "Protecting human rights means

---

[14] "Pollution eats into India's marble glory", *The Times*, February 1, 1992.

[15] "Secrecy Said to Impede Research on Radiation Hazards," *The Washington Post*, May 8, 1992.

preserving the environment, and safeguarding the environment means respecting human rights."[16]

Collaboration between the two communities has the capacity to reinforce and expand the considerable energies of each, and we hope that this joint report is but the first of a series of efforts to work together.

We anticipate closer cooperation in specific campaigns to protect the rights of those at work defending the earth. For example, action alerts aimed at the thousands of members of human rights and environmental groups worldwide about cases such as Wangari Maathai's in Kenya and Father Nery Lito Satur's in the Philippines can be an effective lever for generating pressure on the governments involved to respect the human rights of environmental advocates. Human rights and environmental organizations could also build upon Principle 10 of the draft Rio Declaration to make rights of access to environmental information effective and enforceable at both the national and international levels.

Mexican writer and environmental leader Homero Aridjis eloquently expressed the challenge before us in a recent talk when he declared, "business as usual will not ensure enjoyment of human and environmental rights by our descendants...without rights to information and fair participation in the judicial process it will be impossible to guarantee the right to a healthy environment no matter how many decrees or proclamations are issued by our leaders."[17]

Gara LaMarche
Human Rights Watch

S. Jacob Scherr
Natural Resources Defense Council

---

[16] Cited in "Earth Rights and Responsibilities" Report.

[17] *Ibid.*

BRAZIL

Rural Violence and the Rainforest

Chico Mendes did not learn the word "ecologist" until relatively late in his life, but he really had been one all along. Before the mid-1980s he would probably have described himself only as a labor leader, who with his fellow *seringueiros*, or rubber tappers, was trying to build a successful union in their far corner of the Amazon basin.

But the struggle of the rubber tappers propelled them into contact with the international ecology movement, which explains why worldwide publicity followed the assassination of Chico Mendes on December 22, 1988. The tappers had tried to protect the rain forest, proposing to set aside sections of it as "extractive reserves" in which they could continue to earn their livelihoods in harmony with nature, harvesting rubber latex and Brazil nuts, and shooting wild pigs and other game at sustainable levels.

The rubber tappers believe that the trees respond to the touch of individuals. One experienced tapper explained: "Every time a new tapper starts cutting a rubber tree, the tree has to get used to the guy. Otherwise the tree doesn't produce very well. A tree feels who's doing the cutting. Every tapper has his own style."[1]

These demands for conservation brought them in direct conflict with the landlords, who cleared the rain forest to extract its timber and burned it to replace the towering 20-story trees with cattle pasture. After the green forest canopy is ripped off, the thin underlying soil is washed away by the driving tropical rainstorms. What is left is an ecological desert. In 1987, swaths of the rain forest one and one-half times the size of Czechoslovakia were burned.[2]

---

[1] Andrew Revkin, *The Burning Season,* (Boston: Houghton Mifflin, 1990), p. 71.

[2] Alex Shoumatoff, *The World is Burning,* (Boston: Little Brown, 1990), p.128.

The killing of Chico Mendes was only the most well-known of the 1,681 murders of rural workers and others involved in the struggle over land in Brazil that took place from January 1, 1964 through January 31, 1992. Most of the killings happen with impunity. The Pastoral Land Commission (*Commissão Pastoral de Terra, CPT*) estimates that trials have taken place in only 26 cases, and a mere 15 ended with the conviction of some of the defendants.[3]

The numbers demonstrate that the Brazilian justice system has failed totally to deter violence directed against rural workers and landless peasants. In the year since Americas Watch published a comprehensive report, there has been no discernable improvement in this dismal record.[4]

Even the effort to prosecute the killers of Chico Mendes, which was at first viewed as a promising break with the tradition of impunity, has more recently taken an ambiguous turn. Due to the intense international interest, the alleged killers were arrested and tried within two years. In December 1990, a jury in Xapuri, Acre state, convicted the confessed triggerman, Darci Alves Pereira, and his rancher father, Darly Alves da Silva, who had frequently opposed Mendes and the Rubber Tappers Union. They were each sentenced to nineteen years in prison.

But on February 28, 1992, the appellate court in Rio Branco, Acre, by a two-to-one vote, reversed the father's conviction for planning the murder and ordered a new trial. The lawyers for the Mendes family have appealed the decision to the Supreme Court, in order to avoid a new trial. Until then, the senior Alves, who also faces charges of murdering three people in the state of Paraná in 1978, should remain in

---

[3]The CPT, an organization linked to the National Conference of Brazilian Bishops (*Conferência Nacional dos Bispos do Brasil, CNBB*) was formed by the Catholic Church in 1975 to monitor human rights abuses in Brazil's countryside and to serve and assist landless peasants and rural workers.

[4]See Americas Watch, *Rural Violence in Brazil,* (New York: Human Rights Watch, 1991).

prison. (The conviction of the son was not overturned because he had confessed to the actual killing.)[5]

Many rural organizers, however, fear that the wrong message has already been sent. Benebita Esteves, a spokesperson for the Xapuri Rubbers Tappers Union, said, "With this decision, ranchers across the Amazon won't feel so worried about picking up their shotguns and killing anyone who stands in their way."[6]

LAND REFORM AND THE ENVIRONMENT

The June 1992 United Nations Conference on Environment and Development in Rio de Janeiro should emphasize the relation between the degradation of the environment and the parallel degradation of human rights. Environmental advocates and marginalized subsistence farmers face the same adversary: the large landowners who want to do what they wish with their land and who will fight any efforts at land reform with violence.

Brazil has one of the most unequal concentrations of land ownership in the world. In 1989, the large estates of more than 5000 hectares in size covered half the land.[7] At the opposite end of the scale, three million tiny plots, each averaging only 3.25 hectares, constituted less than three per cent of the country's farmland.[8] This lopsided land ownership pattern contributes to Brazil's extremely unequal distribution of income: in 1989, the wealthiest 20 per cent of Brazil's households

---

[5]Todd Lewan, "Brazil Court Orders New Trial for Rancher Convicted of Killing Chico Mendes," *Associated Press*, February 28, 1992.

[6]*Ibid.*

[7]One hectare equals 2.47 acres.

[8]Secretária de Planejamento e Coordinação da Presidência da República and Fundação Instituto Brasileiro de Geografia e Estatística (IBGE), *Anuário Estatístico de Brasil, 1989*(Rio de Janeiro: IBGE, 1989), p. 293.

accounted for 62.6 per cent of the nation's total income, while the bottom 20 per cent earned only 2.4 per cent.[9]

The unequal landholding pattern persists on the Amazon frontier, even though land there is more plentiful; the two decades of military dictators who relinquished power in 1985 handed out tax breaks and incentives to big landowners.

Big landowners are mostly absentee, with few emotional ties to their holdings. They log the timber for export and destroy the forests, often by burning, to clear pasture for cattle. Their foremen hire large teams of workers to follow the bulldozers through the rain forests, clearing everything in their wide paths. Because the owners can get away with breaking practically every protective labor law, the cost of hiring the large work gangs is incredibly low.

The Brazilian government has also used the Amazon frontier as a safety valve to relieve social pressure in already long-settled rural areas. Government-promoted migration is a substitute for the long overdue land reforms. Jose Lutzenberger, the Brazilian agronomist and ecologist who until recently was his nation's Minister of the Environment, has explained how thousands of poor peasants from southern Brazil migrated up into the Amazon's Rondonia region in the early 1980s after large landowners in their own areas had dispossessed them. He testified that there was "in fact no shortage of land...except the shortages created by the concentration of land holdings."[10]

Deforestation increased, Lutzenberger explained, because the colonizers got titles to their land only after they cleared it. He said: "It is quite common to see settlers give up their clearings after their first meager harvest. They have to make new clearings every year. Then, when the whole plot is cleared, they move on again."[11]

---

[9]The World Bank, *World Development Report 1991*(Washington, D.C.: World Bank, 1991), p. 263.

[10]Susan George, *A Fate Worse than Debt,* (New York: Grove, 1988), pp. 164-5.

[11]*Ibid.*

The various rural organizations that struggle peacefully for land reform in Brazil include ecology as part of their programs. It is, after all, clearly in their interest to conserve the productivity of the plots of land they hope to be able to work if some of the larger holdings are broken up. People who have a stake in their land, whether individual families or members of larger cooperatives, tend not to misuse it like large, indifferent, absentee landlords.

The 1987 Brundtland Report straightforwardly endorses land reform as good ecology. The report says, "Conserving the agricultural resource base and livelihood security of the poor can be mutually supportive...Secure resources and adequate livelihoods lead to good husbandry and sustainable management."[12]

THE VIOLENCE IN RURAL BRAZIL CONTINUES

Americas Watch, in a forthcoming update of its March 1991 report, surveyed human rights abuses in four rural areas of Brazil: Pará in the north, Maranhão in the northeast, Mato Grosso do Sul in the midwest, and Paraná in the south. The update, entitled *The Struggle for Land in Brazil: Rural Violence Continues*, follows a return visit by Americas Watch in November 1991.

The latest survey did not find any substantial improvement. It concludes that "impunity -- or government failure to enforce criminal laws, permitting and encouraging further criminal behavior in the context of the struggle for land -- exists in these regions and throughout Brazil."

The continuing danger had already been tragically underscored on February 4, 1991, just as the first Americas Watch report was being released. A gunman shot Expedito Ribeiro de Souza, a Rural Workers leader in Rio Maria, Pará state. Ribeiro had been receiving death threats, and he had asked, in vain, for police protection.[13]

---

[12]The World Commission on Environment and Development, *Our Common Future*, (New York: Oxford, 1987), p. 129.

[13]Nucleo de Estudos do Violência, Universidade de São Paulo.

Ribeiro's death was quickly followed by the attempted murder of the man who succeeded him as local union president. Federal police protection was provided to three surviving Rio Maria union leaders for a few months, then discontinued for three months. It was only restored after enormous pressure from the Attorney General's office (*Procurador Geral da Justiça*), and from overseas.

The total number of killings tabulated by the Pastoral Land Commission in the struggle for land was fewer in 1991 than in 1990: fifty-one compared to seventy-five.[14] But it is too early to declare that the trend is consistently downward. Some of the decrease in killings is probably due to increased press attention, both in Brazil and abroad, especially after the murder of Chico Mendes. The number of prosecutions each year is so low that it appears to have little deterrent effect on the number of killings.

---

[14] CPT, *Relação dos Assassinatos no Campo*, (CPT Nacional, 1991).

Year	Killings	Prosecutions	Convictions	Conflicts
1985	125	0	0	636
1986	105	0	0	634
1987	109	3	0	582
1988	93	6	4	621
1989	56	3	1	500
1990	75	5	5	401
1991	54	6	4	383

The level of injuries, death threats and evictions where force is used fluctuates as well. In 1991, there were eighty-eight people wounded in conflicts over land, 253 people threatened with death, 2,286 families evicted with judicial orders, and 413 families expelled from their lands illegally.[15] In 1990, 130 people were wounded, 190 were threatened with death, 2,544 families were evicted by judicial order, and 1,681 families were evicted illegally.[16]

In this atmosphere of chronic violence, threats alone are often enough. The warnings usually begin as rumors; anonymous telephone calls or letters are not the practice in rural Brazil. Rather, in the style described by Gabriel Garcia Márquez in his *Chronicles of a Death Foretold*, rumors circulate until everyone in the community is aware that a certain person is marked for death. Often, people will take heed of the warnings and abandon their political or union activities and even leave town.

There is at least one bright spot in Brazil. The federal Attorney General (*Procurador Geral da República*), who has a quasi-independent

[15] Letter from CPT documentation center, April 27, 192. See also CPT, *Conflitos No Campo-Brazil 1991, Terra, Agua E Paz-Viver é um Direito* (Goiania, Goiás: CPT, April 1992).

[16] CPT, *Espinhoso Caminho para a Liberdade: Conflitos no Campo-1990* (Goiania, Goiás: CPT Nacional, April 1991), tables 3 & 4.

constitutional position, is an exception to the otherwise dismal picture of impunity.[17]

Aristides Junqueira, the current Attorney General, and his first Assistant Attorney General (*Sub-Procurador*), Alvaro Ribeiro Costa, have been praised by non-governmental organizations concerned about rural violence. They do respond to the complaints community groups and unions have lodged about the lack of prosecution of various crimes and the lack of federal police protection when crimes are threatened. Attorney General Junqueira has instructed the assistant attorneys general under his jurisdiction to follow through on these complaints.

But the rest of the Brazilian government is not nearly as responsive. The Attorney General and his staff have not had great success in moving the federal Ministry of Justice and the federal police, who are under the jurisdiction of the Ministry of Justice, forward on the question of rural violence. In 1991, during Attorney General Junqueira's second term in office, he even complained publicly to the federal Congressional Inquiry Committee on Rural Violence (*Comissão Parlamentar de Inquérito de Violência no Campo*) that the federal police had not acted in a number of cases of rural violence that he had repeatedly brought to their attention.[18]

---

[17] He or she is named by the President after his or her name is approved by a majority of the federal Senate. The two-year term may be extended but the Attorney General may not be dismissed by the President without the authorization of a majority of the Senate (Constitution, art. 128). The Attorney General is the head of the Public Ministry (*Ministério Público*), which represents the state in penal actions, among other things (Constitution, art. 129).

[18] "Junqueira accusa DPF de omissão nos crimes agrários," *Jornal do Brasil*, November 8, 1991. The federal CPI, an official congressional investigation commission headed by Deputy Roberto Rollemberg of Sao Paulo (PMDB), was formed to investigate the causes and consequences of rural violence throughout Brazil. During the 180 days of its existence, it held more than twenty public meetings and traveled to five states to investigate specific denunciations. However, the CPI was not empowered to draft legislation or conduct criminal investigations, and its activities were boycotted by conservative members of Congress. Various state legislatures have also formed their own CPI's to investigate rural violence.

CONCLUSION: THE LAST TESTAMENT OF CHICO MENDES

Rural Brazil is disfigured by systematic human rights abuses. The big landlords maintain their economic and social power by coercion, resorting to violence if necessary, with the confidence that the chance of retribution is almost non-existent. The continuation of the big landlord system helps to promote the mass destruction of the environment that has rightly drawn world attention. In Brazil, there will be no safeguarding of the environment until the rule of law is brought to the backlands.

Like so many other activists, Chico Mendes knew that he was a marked man. A month before his death, he returned to his frontier town of Xapuri for the last time. As the rumored threats circulated more urgently through the dusty streets, he took time out from organizing to write a farewell:[19]

"I don't want flowers on my grave because I know they'll have been pulled up from the forest. But I'd at least like my murder to serve to put an end to the impunity of the gunmen who have already killed people like me, leaders of the rubber tappers who are pledged to defend the Amazon forest and make of it an example that it is possible to progress without destroying."

---

[19] Alex Shoumatoff, *The World is Burning*, (Boston: Little Brown, 1990), p. 104.

ERITREA

A War on the Environment

Eritrea suffers from an ecological crisis that is perhaps the most severe on the African continent, locked in a cycle of drought and ecological degradation that threatens its ability ever to support its population of between three and four million people. But contrary perhaps to popular perceptions in the West, Eritrea's situation is only in part a natural calamity. A major reason why Eritrea faces ecological disaster is the systematic abuse of human rights by successive Ethiopian governments, which ruled Eritrea between 1962 until their defeat by the forces of the Eritrean People's Liberation Front (EPLF) in May 1991. The decades-long war conducted by the state, operating on a fragile and complex environmental system, has devastated the countryside.

Throughout the highlands, the Eritrean landscape is largely treeless. Water erosion from the brief summer rains has left many fields deeply gullied, with the topsoil washed away to reveal bare stony ground. In the lowlands, wind erosion is contributing to advancing desertification. The water table is falling throughout the country, so that even the capital, Asmara, is frequently left without water. It is possible that tracts of Eritrea will become uninhabitable in the coming years, and the most optimistic environmental scientists talk of halting the degradation in decades at best.

Drought has played its part; whether the recent dry decades have been caused by regular oscillations in the climatic cycle or by a secular change possibly related to global warming remains a matter of dispute. Over-exploitation of the land has also played its part; farmland is over-cultivated, pastures are over-grazed, and the once-plentiful forests are disappearing to provide timber and firewood. The decline in vegetative cover may in turn cause a decrease in convection rainfall.

After thirty years of continuous warfare, it is difficult to reconstruct how the Eritrean economy functions in a "normal" period. Nevertheless, a picture can be pieced together from the few studies of the economy that have been undertaken. It is apparent that Eritrea has always had limited resources, requiring a delicate balance between society and the environment and traditional practices of resource conservation. Eritrean farmers and herders had developed a well-adjusted set of strategies for managing the limited resources of their country, exploiting its diversity and conserving the productivity of the land.

The Eritrean economy is based upon a mixture of farming, herding and trade. A study by the University of Leeds, Britain, estimated that locally-grown food could provide about seven and a half months' consumption needs in a "normal, peacetime" year, falling to less than five months' needs in a "normal, wartime" year.[1] The balance is made good by animal rearing, trade and local crafts and industry.

Over the centuries, rural Eritreans had established means of living in and exploiting their inhospitable environment. The ownership of livestock was particularly important. In the lowlands, the majority of people subsist from pastoralism, and in the highlands, even those normally categorized as farmers rely heavily on animals, for milk, sale and for rearing plow oxen. All animal herders were required to be mobile, moving their herds according to the season and the rainfall (markedly different rainfall regimes prevail in different parts of the country). No single area could support the herds all year round, so semi-nomadism was both essential and efficient for utilizing the resources that existed. Similarly, farming practices were adapted to local conditions, employing regular fallow periods and other means for retaining soil fertility.

Historically, Eritrea has always imported food from Sudan and Ethiopia, by exporting animals, salt (mined near the Red Sea coast), gum, incense and manufactures. Eritrean traders remain active throughout the region, using pack animals, vehicles and boats.

---

[1] Lars Bondestam, Lionel Cliffe and Philip White, "Eritrea: Food and Agricultural Production Assessment Study, Final Report," Leeds, 1988.

THIRTY YEARS OF WAR

In September 1961, the first armed confrontation occurred between the Eritrean Liberation Front (ELF) and the Ethiopian army. In 1967, in its first major campaign, the Ethiopian army burned over 320 villages, mainly in the lowlands, confiscated or slaughtered over 70,000 domestic animals, and killed at least 640 civilians. 25,000 refugees fled to Sudan.[2] The population from the destroyed villages was regrouped in large security hamlets or protected villages, where they were kept under close surveillance.

In 1970, a second major offensive led to another round of killing, burning and forced displacement. However, the most intense hostilities were reserved for the period beginning in 1975, a year that saw a further round of killing and destruction, that for the first time encompassed substantial areas of the Eritrean highlands.

What had been a guerrilla war turned into a large-scale conventional war in 1978, when the Ethiopian army, enlarged and re-equipped with massive Soviet assistance, began a series of offensives against the ELF and a second breakaway front, the EPLF. The ELF was defeated and the EPLF was pushed back into a mountainous enclave in the northeastern province of Sahel. The following ten years saw ten major offensives, the largest of which deployed over 120,000 regular troops, with armored divisions and air support, to attack the EPLF positions. The war was a unique example of conventional trench warfare in the contemporary world, in which the Ethiopian forces used sustained artillery and air bombardments, followed by massed infantry attacks, to dislodge the Eritreans. Casualties were enormous on both sides, but the EPLF was not dislodged.

In 1988, the EPLF was able to turn to the offensive, and in a series of large-scale battles over the following three years, defeated the Ethiopian army and won independence in May 1991.

---

[2] For details on this offensive and subsequent military actions in Eritrea, see Africa Watch, *Evil Days: 30 Years of War and Famine in Ethiopia*, September 1991.

THE DIRECT IMPACT OF COMBAT

The most obvious impact on the natural environment is the physical damage caused by bombardment and mechanized attacks. Innumerable trees and hillsides are scarred with the impact of shells or bombs; pastures and woods bear the marks of burning with napalm or phosphorous. Mechanized forces have flattened all vegetation where they have been. One observer described a battlefield in 1978:

> The valley was full of tanks, dead bodies and trucks from edge to edge. All the dry grass was burned totally, and rows of trees were [knocked] down from the tanks. The planes never stopped coming. They were dropping different types of bombs including napalm, and at times the valley was so filled with smoke you couldn't see.[3]

The construction of defensive emplacements also caused damage to the environment. During the long decade of semi-stalemate (1978-88), the front lines scarcely moved across the north-eastern mountains. Trenches and fortifications were constructed over several hundred kilometers from Nacfa in the north to Halhal, near Keren in the south. Many of the already-scarce trees that grew in this dry area were chopped down to use in the construction.

The EPLF forces lived largely underground, in caves, to shelter from the day-in-day-out aerial bombardment. The Ethiopian garrisons, with many more troops, requisitioned residential areas of the Eritrean towns, and also constructed their own quarters, for enlisted men and hangers on (many of whom were women taken either under false pretenses or by force to serve as the soldiers' sexual servants). The garrisons' appetite for construction and firewood further accelerated the destruction of Eritrea's forests.

Deforestation was also pursued as military policy, on the grounds that forests provided cover for guerrilla fighters. For this reason, many trees were cleared in the vicinity of garrisons, to provide open lines of fire. Many eucalyptus trees from the Biet Giorgis woods around Asmara

---

[3] Quoted in *Horn of Africa*, 4.1, 1981, p. 22.

were cut down when the city was besieged in the mid-1970s. Large areas of forest in the coastal plains of Semhar were put to the torch a few years later, for the same reason.

Effects of Forced Relocations and Restrictions on Movement

As well as the direct effects from the actual armed conflict, there were also more insidious consequences for the environment stemming from the impact of the government's counter-insurgency strategies on the economic activities of the rural population. The government employed various policies of forced relocation and restrictions on movement as a means of controlling the civilian population. As a general rule, these practices impoverished the population and compelled people to abandon long-established land management systems and turn to activities that caused environmental damage. The traditional delicate balance that had been established between the population and the natural environment was upset, with disastrous consequences.

The most obviously damaging counter-insurgency strategy was forcible relocation. Starting from the 1967 campaign, until the late 1980s, rural people were compelled to abandon their villages to live under military surveillance in larger communities. The need to rebuild wooden houses was itself damaging to the environment. The imposition of curfews and regular attendance checks in the controlled villages, and the difficulty of obtaining travel permits, greatly restricted the distances that people could travel to collect firewood or to find grazing for their animals. A semi-nomadic lifestyle which ranged broadly but lightly over great distances is necessary in a region of such sparse natural resources. The effects of these restrictions were therefore predictable -- each of these militarized villages was quickly surrounded by a circle of total despoliation.

The relocation policy forced many rural people to abandon activities that had played a vital role in their subsistence. Semi-nomadic herding of animals became impossible for villagers; pack animals could no longer be grazed at night and so their owners had to buy grass to feed them, or else sell them. Water shortages in some areas compelled herders to abandon livestock rearing altogether. The collecting of wild fruits and petty trading between villages also had to be abandoned.

The immediate result was that farming had to be intensified. Because outlying fields could no longer be cultivated, pressure of cultivation on the nearby fields was increased. Strategies for preserving the topsoil could not be maintained. Fallows were abandoned and hillslopes cleared for planting, accelerating erosion.

The increasing insufficiency of farming and animal herding as a means of survival led some of the population to rely more on non-farming activities, which in turn had adverse ecological effects. Impoverished households in countries such as Eritrea have few options to fall back upon, notably the selling of firewood, charcoal and fodder. To engage in these low-level trading activities, poor people turned to mining the natural environment; throughout Eritrea it has become common to see destitute rural people destroying what little remains of the tree cover, in order to meet the overriding need to feed themselves.

Related to the policy of forced relocation was the systematic imposition of restrictions on movement. Roadblocks were instituted, ostensibly to prevent potential recruits joining the rebels, guerrillas infiltrating behind government lines and sympathizers taking supplies to the rebels. But the roadblocks also served to prevent migrant labor and trade. The clampdown on trade blocked the import of timber, firewood and charcoal from more thickly forested regions of Ethiopia, forcing people to turn to the trees in their locality for construction and fuel. Taking punitive measures against people found travelling without an official permit had the same effect. As a result, more and more essential economic options for the rural poor were stripped away, leading inevitably to greater and greater dependence on the land.

Those who managed to migrate constituted an environmental problem of their own. About 500,000 Eritreans fled to neighboring Sudan as refugees. The impact of this huge number of destitute people on eastern Sudan was devastating. Like their impoverished countrymen at home, Eritrean refugees in Sudan were unable to follow sensible resource management practices, and instead stripped bare the areas they were obliged to inhabit for housing, firewood and a meager income. With the victory of the EPLF, they are now returning home, adding to the population of destitutes; unless given relief assistance or economic opportunities, they too will try to scratch a living by selling wood.

Another related policy with devastating consequences has been the use of landmines. Landmines have been used by both sides in the Eritrean war to defend military positions, but the government also used them to restrict population movements. For example, a closely guarded militarized village might have only one permitted entrance, all the others being planted with anti-personnel landmines. Large areas have therefore been placed out of bounds by the fact that they are seeded with landmines or -- equally devastatingly from an economic point of view -- that people believe they may be mined, and so will not use them. While these areas are "protected" from human exploitation, the fact that they cannot be used drives people to overuse and abuse other areas instead.

REPRESSION AND THE ENVIRONMENTAL DEBATE IN ETHIOPIA AND ERITREA

Another casualty of the war, and the political repression associated with it, has been sensible debate on the natural environment in Ethiopia and Eritrea, and what policies might be followed to ameliorate the situation. The former Ethiopian government of Colonel Mengistu Haile Mariam turned the environmental lobby to its political advantage, using environmental protection as a justification to conduct counter-insurgency measures or to extend government power in the rural areas.

The inevitable consequence was widespread rural antipathy and active resistance to any form of government-sponsored conservation efforts. Farmers recruited to plant trees in government forest reserves were known to place them in the ground upside-down, as silent resistance to a government that had confiscated their land without compensation for the reserves, and also in protests of the fact that they would never gain any benefits from the trees, which would be managed and felled by the government. Peasant opposition to these supposed conservation schemes contributed to the revolt that forced the government from power, and hopefully will in turn force the new governments in both Eritrea and Ethiopia to adopt much more participatory policies of environmental protection.

Information on the environment has been suppressed for political reasons. Under former governments in Ethiopia, rainfall records have been kept secret. The government frequently needed to claim international relief assistance for famine-stricken populations, and drought was the most convenient culprit, whereas the reality has more often been that army activities or agricultural policies were to blame. False claims of drought having caused famine were made in 1980 and 1983, and the government Relief and Rehabilitation Commission (RRC) falsely claimed that "there have scarcely been any real rains in the drought-prone areas since the 1972-4 catastrophe."[4] Had rainfall records been public, this pretense could have been debunked.

Similar considerations led to tight restrictions on research into sensitive topics. Only a few researchers, hand-picked for their loyalty and ideological correctness, were allowed to investigate and report on a controversial scheme to relocate 600,000 peasants forcibly from the dry northern highlands to the more fertile southern and western lowlands. Their conclusion was, not surprisingly, positive. A less fortunate Ethiopian research team that tried to do field research on resettlement found itself detained by regional authorities.

Environmental arguments were adduced in favor of all these government land-management programs. In support of the resettlement from the highlands, the RRC made the highly misleading claim that "the fact is that much of northern Ethiopia, particularly the northern provinces...[are] today an uninhabitable wasteland,"[5]. Similar claims were echoed by some western environmentalists, sensitive to Ethiopia's ecological predicament but blind to government's complicity in the crisis.[6]

To the extent that they have been possible, independent investigations have shown that in fact the resettlement program had

---

[4]RRC, *The Challenges of Drought: Ethiopia's Decade of Struggle in Relief and Rehabilitation*, Addis Ababa, (1985) p. 231.

[5]RRC, 1985, p. 180.

[6]See, for example, Graham Hancock, *Ethiopia: The Challenge of Hunger*, (London, 1985).

negative environmental consequences.[7] In combination with other arbitrary and violent government policies, resettlement increased insecurity among farmers in the north, deterring them from improving their land. The planting of trees and construction of terraces were undoubtedly impeded by farmers' fears of land confiscation. Moreover, the resettlement began the destruction of the ecosystem in the south, raising fears of a new environmental crisis coming to a head within a decade.

An invidious result of this and other policies pursued with an alleged environmental justification has been the debasing of ecological discourse in Ethiopia and Eritrea. Rural people are now justifiably skeptical of environmental protection programs planned and implemented without their full participation, consent and control.

CONCLUSION

The war in Eritrea and its offshoots -- the human rights abuses directed against civilians and the politically motivated distortion of environmental policy -- forced the populace to abandon long-standing traditional practices that allowed them to survive in a precarious ecology. Three decades of human rights abuses have left not only hundreds of thousands of people dead, but a fragile natural environment grossly and perhaps irretrievably misused.

---

[7] Alemneh Dejene, *Environment, Famine and Politics in Ethiopia, A View from the Village*, (Boulder, Co., 1990).

INDIA

Before the Deluge

Since 1988, rural activists and social and political action groups in western India have campaigned against the construction of a series of dams on the Narmada river, one of the largest of which is known as the Sardar Sarovar Project (SSP). Activists associated with these groups, particularly those from the Narmada Bachao Andolan (NBA, Save the Narmada Movement)[1] who have organized or participated in demonstrations against the project have been subjected to arbitrary arrest, illegal detention, beatings and other forms of physical abuse. These abuses appear to be part of an increasingly repressive campaign by the state governments involved to prevent the groups from organizing support for the protests in villages affected by the dam and disseminating information about the environmental and social consequences of the project.

In 1985, the World Bank approved $450 million for the construction of the Sardar Sarovar dam,[2] one of the first large dams of the series. The other major foreign funder, Japan, decided to withdraw its Official Development Assistance (ODA), in May 1990, as a result of a campaign by Japanese environmental groups highlighting the adverse social and environmental effects of the project.[3] In late 1991, growing

---

[1]A loose affiliation of groups from all over India, with the core comprising three groups from each of the affected states: Narmada Dharangrastha Samiti (Organization of the Narmada Dam-Affected People) from Maharashtra, Narmada Navnirman Samiti (Organization for a New Life on the Narmada) in Madhya Pradesh, and Narmada Asargrastha Samiti (Organization of People Affected by the Narmada Dam) in Gujarat.

[2]This constitutes approximately 10 percent of the total amount needed for the dam.

[3]According to a report in *Tokyo Shimbun* on May 23, 1990, "a discontinuation of ODA after construction has already begun is exceptional. The decision is due in part to a review of the carelessness of environmental and cultural impact

opposition to the project prompted World Bank authorities to commission an independent team to evaluate concerns raised about the dam.

Construction of the dam has continued, however, and the first submergence of villages in Maharashtra is scheduled to begin with the onset of the monsoon in July 1992. Manibeli, a village in Maharashtra near the Gujarat border, is expected to be one of the first villages to be flooded. Because of this status, it has become the target of demonstrations by those protesting the dam and the focus of particularly blatant police abuse. Protests increased in July-August 1991 when officials came to Manibeli and other villages to tell residents that they were going to be submerged and they would have to leave. Since then, the police have attempted to stop activists from entering the village, and have resorted to frequent detentions and intimidation of villagers. There is fear that in the months before the scheduled submergence, confrontations in the village could escalate, resulting in further human rights abuses.

BACKGROUND

The Narmada Valley Project (NVP), of which the Sardar Sarovar dam is a part, is one of the largest such projects ever undertaken anywhere in the world. The entire project proposes the eventual construction of 30 large dams, 135 medium-sized dams and some 3,000 smaller dams along the Narmada river and its tributaries. An estimated 248 towns and villages are scheduled to be submerged, and at least 90,000 people relocated by the Sardar Sarovar alone.[4]

The project has been controversial from the outset. It was launched in 1946 when the governments of the Central Provinces and Bombay initiated a number of studies to explore the potential for electric power generation and irrigation on the Narmada river system. In 1961 the Sardar Sarovar Project (SSP) was inaugurated. Initial negotiations

---

assessments conducted prior to the project's start." Asia Watch sources believe Japan is reconsidering funding for the project in 1992.

[4]Most of those affected belong to tribal communities which have traditionally depended on the river and forest land around it for their livelihood.

among the three states failed to resolve disputes over the height of the dam and the distribution of water and power. Continuing disagreements led the central government to establish the Narmada Water Disputes Tribunal (NWDT) to mediate among the states.[5] In 1978 the World Bank entered into negotiations with the Narmada Planning Group and finalized an agreement to begin funding in 1985.

In 1980, the government ordered additional studies to clear the project for "environmental soundness and sustainability," as required under a new Forest Conservation Act. At first, the Ministry of Environment and Forests (MOEF) released a report which found that the project had not met the environmental requirements. But the MOEF came under severe political pressure for its decision; in April 1987 it released the project subject to fulfillment of a number of conditions, including carrying out field surveys, completing the rehabilitation plan and determining the seismicity of the site.[6] The decision provoked protests from a wide spectrum of social and political action groups who called for a review of the whole project on the grounds that the government had violated both the provisions of the NWDT and its own laws in the manner in which the project had received clearance. The groups also demanded that the World Bank cease funding the project until the concerns were addressed. Demonstrations during this period resulted in widespread arrests.

By 1991, growing frustration with the government's refusal to consider the demands of the groups for a thorough review prompted them to expand their campaign of demonstrations and grass-roots

---

[5]It determined that (1) Gujarat was to pay for the cost of land acquisition and rehabilitation of all dislocated persons from Madhya Pradesh and Maharashtra and (2) any family (every 'major son' was to be treated as a separate family unit) losing more than 25% of its holding was entitled to five acres of irrigation land.

[6]By August 1990, however, the Environment Subgroup of the Narmada Control Authority concluded that, "In the absence of a definite time frame for each of these studies, surveys or action plans, the implementation of the requisite safeguards and action plans pari-passu with the construction of engineering works would obviously not be possible. Under the circumstances, the approval granted must be deemed to have lapsed."

mobilization to include acts of civil disobedience against the state governments and the corporation administering the SSP. That campaign, which continues to this day, has resulted in widespread abuses against activists and villagers in the affected area. According to Asia Watch sources, since mid-1991 more than 1,000 people have been detained for periods ranging from several days to several weeks.

ABUSES AGAINST ACTIVISTS AND VILLAGERS IN THE DAM PROJECT SITE

Leading activists have been subjected to repeated short-term detention, frequently under laws which provide for preventive detention. In many cases, they have been detained for periods ranging from several days or longer without being produced before a magistrate as required under Indian law. During mass arrests at demonstrations and rallies in villages surrounding the dam site, protesters have been beaten with canes, or otherwise assaulted by the police, in some cases sustaining severe injuries. Peaceful demonstrations have also been tear-gassed.

Asia Watch is aware of the government's right to counter any legitimate threat to the peace by enforcement of the law. We are also aware that some of the charges brought against activists associated with the anti-dam movement include acts of violence.[7] However, in the vast majority of cases investigated, the police of the three state governments involved have routinely resorted to the use of excessive force to break up legitimate, peaceful gatherings and to intimidate activists and local villagers involved in the opposition campaign. They have also misused preventive detention laws to detain people for the peaceful expression of their views. Even in cases where the police have had grounds to arrest persons engaged in acts of civil disobedience, the police have routinely abused detainees in custody and have violated laws requiring detainees to be produced promptly before a magistrate and allowing them access to family and legal counsel.

---

[7]For example, Asia Watch is aware of reports that on April 9 or 10, 1992, police who threatened to shoot a demonstrator were told by the other residents that if he did so, no police would leave the village alive. One woman reportedly threw stones, although none apparently struck any police officer.

In addition, since October 1988, the Official Secrets Act (OSA) has been in force in villages in the submergence zone and around the dam construction site. Under this law, the central or state government may declare any place to be "prohibited" if it considers that "information with respect thereto or the destruction or obstruction thereof or interference therewith would be useful to an enemy." Offenses punishable with up to 14 years' imprisonment include approaching, inspecting, passing over or being in the vicinity of any prohibited place "for any purpose prejudicial to the safety or interests of the State." The Act also makes "the disclosure, communication, possession or receipt of any official information" with imprisonment up to three years, or a fine, or both. What is meant by "official information" may cover any "sketch, plan, model article, note, document or information which relates to or is used in a prohibited place or relates to anything in such a place." On its face, the law violates Article 19 of the International Covenant on Civil and Political Rights which guarantees the right to "seek, receive and impart information and ideas of all kinds."

Girish Patel, a senior lawyer in the Gujarat High Court and former dean of the law school of Gujarat University, who has challenged the Act's validity, observed that

> We do not know which information, which plan, which document, etc. will bring us under the clutches of the Act...our discussion with the deputy superintendent of police confirmed our apprehensions that the authorities are using or abusing the provisions of the Official Secrets Act to inhibit the democratic activities of the people in the project area.

On January 30, 1989, NBA activists organized a demonstration against the Official Secrets Act. Eighteen activists were arrested, including Girish Patel, and charged with offenses under the act. The charges were dropped a few months later before the case went to trial. Activists have also been banned from entering villages in the affected area. Under the OSA, access to the construction site and surrounding villages is prohibited and information about the project is subject to government censorship. Labor unions have been denied access to the dam construction workers, and labor activists have been threatened by government officials. As one lawyer told Asia Watch, "Freedom of speech is always a casualty of big development projects. How can you debate and discuss if you cannot find out about it?"

Arrests and Beatings

Since 1990, the NBA's campaign against the dam has led to increased arrests and police brutality against activists and villagers participating in rallies and in acts of civil disobedience. The campaign has included sit-down strikes (*dharnas*) to block roads or construction sites and forming human chains around government offices or officials (*gheraoing*). The major incidents in the Narmada valley during this period demonstrate a pattern of repeated short-term detentions under a preventive detention law (section 151 of the Indian Penal Code or 107 of the Criminal Procedure Code). Under these laws, the detainee must provide security, and if the offense is committed the security is forfeited. The police apparently resort to the frequent use of these laws to obstruct gatherings and prevent activists from participating in demonstrations or meetings. A lawyer interviewed by Asia Watch stated:

> The police routinely file criminal cases against activists as a form of harassment. The first or second time you are charged you may be released on bail. The third time the magistrate may impose conditions, such as restricting the person from visiting the area. In order to get bail the person must accept the conditions or be jailed, sometimes for years.

In addition, the police routinely disregard laws requiring them to inform the detainee of the charges, and whether they are bailable or non-bailable; or permit the detainee to contact his or her family or lawyer. The police also frequently transfer detainees from one jail to another, making it difficult to trace where anyone is being held. In other cases the police simply resort to the use of force to break up gatherings.

Asia Watch investigated a number of incidents of abuses which have occurred since early 1990.

▪ In the town of Barwani, on April 6, 1990, activists launched a demonstration at the NBA office in support of a fast undertaken by NBA leaders and other activists in Bombay. At around noon, they were ordered to disperse, but they refused. The police charged into the group and began arresting the protesters and beating them with canes. Some were dragged to the police jeeps. One of the detained reported: "The officials were saying, 'We'll bury you all.' Now we have been hit so often we no longer care." In all, 150 people were detained, including Baba Amte, the 76-year-old spiritual leader of the movement who is reported to be in frail health and was taken to the hospital. All were released that night, but one man was hospitalized for an eye injury sustained during the beatings, another for an injury to the skull.

- On September 26, 1990, a demonstration was held in the village of Kasravad. Although the organizers had first obtained the permission of the subdivisional magistrate for the rally, police began arresting leading activists from the area on the night of September 25 and held them under section 151 of the Indian Penal Code (IPC). The next day, a large number of police moved into the area and blocked all the roads, preventing people from reaching their homes, possibly as an attempt to prevent NBA leader Medha Patkar from addressing the rally. Prominent activists were detained and prevented from reaching the rally; others went into hiding to avoid arrest. Patkar, who managed to reach the village in spite of police presence, was detained when she arrived in Kasuarad. The detainees were released after three or four days.

- On October 2, 1990, the Chief Minister of Madhya Pradesh, Sundurlal Patwa, arrived in the town of Kukshi to address a public meeting. Before his arrival, police arrested activists in Alirajpur and other villages in the submergence area under section 151 of the IPC. In the nearby village of Kasravad, where the local people had blocked construction of a bridge related to the dam, the main activists in the area were beaten and accused of "attacking the police." They were held for three or four days in the Barwani police station before being released.

- Another rally was planned for November 9, 1990. NBA activists reported that after the authorities were informed of the event, several activists were arrested on November 5 and held for four days under section 151 of the IPC. When they were released they were informed that they would have to report to the police station every month for the next six months.

According to local activists, physical assaults by the police on demonstrators increased markedly after the "Long March" -- a demonstration which lasted from December 25, 1990 to January 31, 1991, during which protestors walked the length of the valley from the eastern-most point of planned submergence to the Gujarat border.

On December 28, four journalists who were covering the march were detained for one and a half hours in the village of Kunwat by the Madhya Pradesh police.[8]

The demonstrators had intended to march on the dam site, but were blocked by the Gujarat police when they reached the state border. On December 28, some 2,000 tribal participants in the march were turned back by the Gujarat police when they reached the state line and were threatened with "dire consequences" if they tried to cross over.[9] Across the border in Gujarat, dam supporters rallied and threatened to stop any activists from entering the state. On January 4, some who had managed to cross the border were pushed back, and 140 were detained.[10] NBA activists in New Delhi filed a habeas corpus petition in the High Court arguing that the police action violated the rights of freedom of movement and association.[11] On January 25, police from Maharashtra and Gujarat charged into the group, arresting scores of demonstrators and beating them with canes.

On the same day, there were arrests and beatings of demonstrators at other sites in the valley and wanton destruction of private property. One activist described the events in Barwani, where local activists staged a support program to protest the lack of response from the government.

---

[8] See "4 Scribes Held, Tribals Sent Back," *Free Press*, (Indore), December 12, 1990.

[9] *Ibid.*

[10] See "140 Anti-Narmada Activists Arrested," *Times of India*, January 5, 1991.

[11] The case was never decided however, because the court allowed the government three weeks to reply and by then the march had ended.

> Women were beaten on their private parts and dragged by the hair on the road. Two or three people were hospitalized. On January 25, Shri Ram from Bagat received a severe head injury from a policeman's blow. He was hospitalized, and the policemen ordered him to be chained to his bed. In all, 41 people were arrested from Barwani that day. The police also broke bullock carts, bicycles, motorscooters. Bullocks were driven off... There were some 150 persons there, including many women and some children. The Dhar Collector [a senior police official], Inder Kumar Sharma, came down from his car and ordered a lathi-charge [breaking up the demonstration by beating the protesters with canes]. The police pulled one boy, Ambala, from a wheelchair and beat him. When the demonstrators fled into nearby houses, the police followed and pulled them out of the houses to beat them.

There was also a protest in the town of Chikaldha on the same day. Although no order to forcibly disperse the protesters was given, activists reported similar incidents of beatings of the demonstrators. The police arrested seven in Chikaldha, including a 75-year-old man, and brought them to the Barwani jail. All seven were struck with canes while being arrested and were also beaten on their legs and backs in the police jeep along the way. All were charged under sections 151 of the IPC. In addition, they were charged with "wrongful restraint and criminal intimidation," for which they had to report to the police station every several months and had to provide a surety of Rs. 5000 (U.S.$200).

- During the census of February-March 1991, the state government of Madhya Pradesh notified those living in villages in the submergence zone that they "did not belong to state." When the census officials came, people in all the affected villages of Madhya Pradesh and Maharashtra organized a boycott. After that the police filed charges against people who had participated from these villages for "coming in the way of government work."

- On April 18, 1991, at about 5:30 or 6:00 p.m. eight NBA activists received a report that two people from Narmada Nagar had been hospitalized at the Barwani hospital after the police had broken up a demonstration. The activists were on their way to Barwani when the police stopped them. According to a young woman activist, N.:

> There were six jeeps, with about fifty police in all...In the police jeep, the police still hit me with their lathis and pulled my hair and slapped me on the way to the Kukshi police station.

Two other male activists who were detained were also hit with canes. When they reached the police station, the two men were ordered to strip and were kept in the jail only in their underwear. That night they were transferred to the Dhar jail and charged under section 151 of the IPC. At 1:00 a.m. all three were produced before the magistrate. However, N. refused food and water and demanded a medical exam, which was ordered after initially being refused. The doctor would not tell her the results of the exam. Under Section 151, a detainee has the right to be released on a personal bond, but the three were held for 7 days.

During this time the two men who had been detained were kept in handcuffs. When they told the SDM that the Supreme Court had prohibited keeping detainees in handcuffs, but he told them, "The courts keep on giving a lot of directives but we don't have to follow them."

Manibeli, the village of some 85 families in a predominantly tribal area of Maharashra, is scheduled to be submerged in 1992. Since mid-1991, villagers have been subjected to increased pressure from government authorities to accept relocation. Because of this pressure, the NBA has stepped up its activities to oppose government efforts to relocate villagers refusing to leave. The authorities have responded by forcibly breaking up demonstrations and detaining scores of protesters.

- On August 3, 1991, 600-700 police entered Manibeli and arrested 79 activists, including three women. At 3:00 a.m. the detainees were brought to Dhule jail. The next day they were produced in court.

According to those detainees interviewed by Asia Watch, tribal detainees were separated from non-tribals despite protests by other detainees.[12] The police reportedly told the other detainees that the tribal detainees had accepted bail, thereby admitting guilt. Sources stated that those who had accepted bail had been forced to put their thumbprints on the bail papers. Four of those released were immediately rearrested and brought back to the jail in handcuffs, where they were kept separate from the other detainees, held in jail for 14 days, (seven before being allowed to see her lawyer), one female reported:

> We kept asking where the four tribal detainees were being held but they would not tell us. In the end they were held for twelve days without anyone being told where they were. All of us were arrested under sections 151 and 144. Some of those detained also had older charges still pending. We were never produced before a magistrate. We were finally released on a court order at about 1:00 a.m. But I was immediately rearrested, even though the police are not permitted to arrest a woman after 6:00 p.m. or to arrest someone from within the jail compound.

On the same day in Barwani, "police created a nuisance by shouting obscenities and curses throughout the night of August 3 outside Baba Amte's hut...he was followed by police and open threats were hurled over loud speakers fitted on police jeeps."[13]

▪ On August 30, 1991, a demonstration was held in Kasravad against the construction of a bridge which forms part of the dam project. When the protesters requested permission from the police to talk to workers at the bridge construction site, the police refused and launched a lathi-charge on the group. Two men were injured in the head. Many others were beaten and some were taken to the hospital. By 4:00 p.m., 90 people had been detained. They were not held inside the jail but were kept instead on the grounds outside the Barwani jail overnight despite

---

[12] Activists in the Narmada valley contend that the local authorities have tried to intimidate tribal villagers involved in the protests in an effort to claim that the opposition is generated by outsiders.

[13] *Economic Times* (Bombay) September 5, 1991.

the monsoon rain. They were then transferred to the Kargoan jail and held for 12 days. One of the detainees told Asia Watch that they were not given any food until after they were transferred to Kargoan jail, and that for the first two or three days after their transfer the police would not tell relatives and others who inquired where they had been taken. According to press reports, "Several were badly beaten and had to be taken to hospital. Over 80 people were arrested. Mounted police then entered Kasravad village, threatened everyone with dire consequences, and dragged women out of their houses by their hair."[14]

After the 90 had been arrested, a large deployment of police entered Kasravad. According to local activists, the police detained the wife of a leading activist named Ismailbhai, saying that "if we take her to jail he'll have to follow." The SP [Superintendent], Ram Nivas, ordered her to go in the police jeep along with her son. The SP then drove with them in the jeep to the house of Baba Amte. The SP told Baba Amte, "I would have ordered my men to shoot on sight; I would have seen the blood of those people." Then he released Ismailbhai's wife and son on the road to walk back to Kasravad.

The 90 detainees were held under section 151. In addition, 33 were charged with "rioting", "unlawful assembly", "wrongful restraint", "mischief", "attempted murder" and "criminal intimidation." The police also alleged that some people had thrown stones. However, to Asia Watch's knowledge, none of those detained was prosecuted for throwing stones, and no one else was later charged with throwing stones although the police were awarded Rs. 500 [U.S.$ 20] in compensation. Following the incident, section 144, which prohibits the assembly of more than five persons, was imposed on Kasravad for a month. After the August 1991 arrests, several activists associated with the NBA were banned from 33 villages in the planned submergence area for the next two months.[15] However, many of the activists defied the ban to continue to work in the area.

---

[14] *Ibid*.

[15] The ban was lifted after the monsoon.

Government surveyors have been a focus of the civil disobedience campaign in the Narmada valley because the surveys of villages in the submergence zone were required to have been carried out before the dam was built. Asia Watch does not question the government's right to arrest persons illegally obstructing roads and other public facilities. However, in many cases the arrests of those protesting the government surveys were accompanied by the excessive use of force by the police, beatings and other forms of physical abuse, humiliating treatment and illegally denying those detained access to lawyers and medical care.

- On November 21, 1991, when government surveyors arrived in Kothra, Dharampuri, a group of 26 men and 26 women began a sit-down strike to block the roads. They were arrested and taken to Dhar jail. On November 22 demonstrators gathered to oppose the detention and staged a protest rally several miles from the survey site. Armed police lathi-charged the demonstrators, injuring a number of protesters. The police arrested seven women -- including two elderly women -- and 35 men and took them to Dhar jail. NBA activists then began another sit-down strike to protest the fact that none of the detainees had been produced before a magistrate. One of the activists described the events as follows:

> At about 4:00 p.m. the SDM [subdivisional magistrate] returned with hundreds of armed police and ordered us to disperse. We told him he could arrest us but our demands still stood. After about five minutes the police formed a cordon around the group and began to beat people and drag them to the police vans, even though we had told them we would go voluntarily. Eighteen women and about 70 men were arrested. Then they had no more room in the vans so they just kept beating the other people. I was dragged by my hair and pushed to the ground. Policemen kicked me in the shoulder and back and hit me with their lathis on my back and arm and slapped me. Then they threw me in the van. They continued to beat us in the vans.They even hit an 82 year old woman, Ratnabhai, from Jalkara village, who fainted. When we asked for water they refused to give us any. One woman, Tarabhen from Katla village, suffered a lot of lathi blows. Another girl, Rakesh, who was 16,

> was badly beaten. The police threatened to push the lathi down her throat and into her vagina. They said to her: "You want to be leaders -- we'll see to it that you can't even speak. We'll see to it that you stop thinking of yourselves as leaders." We learned later that the men had been beaten as well and the police had not permitted them to relieve themselves.

The detainees were taken to the Dharampuri police station. There they were given documents to sign which they were not permitted to read. One of those who had been detained stated:

> I told them we refused to sign unless they told us what we were being charged with. Then they hit me and some others who were refusing to sign...The MLA [member of the legislative assembly] Mr. Jingalal, had been informed and came to the police station and demanded to see me and Dr. Chauhan, another activist. We were permitted to see him. He demanded that the police produce us before a magistrate and have us medically examined, but the police did not do so.

At 10:00 p.m. the detainees were transferred to Dhar jail. By then there were 165 at Dhar jail, including those who had been arrested earlier. None had been produced before a magistrate. On the evening of November 24 several detainees filed a habeas corpus petition on their own behalf and complaints [First Information Reports, or FIRs] against the police. One of the detainees who had drafted the petition said:

> On November 25 the Dhar jailer told us he wanted to get us transferred to the Indore jail. I demanded a copy of the habeas corpus petition and his signature acknowledging receipt of the petition and the FIR. He refused. We were then taken to Indore jail without even being able to tell the others detained where we were going. We were afraid the petition we had submitted would never be filed so we submitted another one from Indore jail.

The detainees who had been transferred to Indore jail were finally produced before the High Court magistrate on November 28. The High Court ordered that they be medically examined. The remaining 163 detainees were not produced until December 1. Those arrested on the November 21 were charged with "threatening government and police officers" and "obstructing a government function." Those arrested on November 22 were charged under section 151 of the IPC, although eight of them were also charged with obstructing a government function. All were released on December 11 but required to report to the police station at monthly intervals. Two reporters from Talwai who were taking photos of the demonstration were detained for a day.

▪ On December 2, 1991, forty-two people were arrested in the village of Gangly for preventing government officials from carrying out a survey of the submergence area. Some of the protestors were beaten while being arrested. According to activists, one man had his arm broken, another required stitches in his head. On December 3, demonstrators assembled at the neighboring village of Ekelbari to oppose government survey work there. When the police lathi-charged the group, the demonstrators fled. On December 6, 20 people were arrested in Bawaria during a protest against survey work there. All were charged under section 151 of the IPC. On December 12, 250 people were arrested in villages along the Narmada river in Madhya Pradesh during government survey work.

On December 31, 1991, residents of Manibeli were served notices to vacate the village by January 31, 1992. At the same time, 27 families in Manibeli returned lease papers assigning them to alternative lands for relocation. Activists with the NBA argue that the provisions of the original Narmada Water Disputes Tribunal award stipulated that notice must be given 18 months before the scheduled submergence. The families have challenged the eviction notices in court, and the case is pending.

▪ Villagers who have rejected the alternative lands provided in compensation have also been detained. According to a report in the *Indian Express*, in March 1992, ten people were reportedly detained as they returned to their village of Vadgam after rejecting a site in the Baroda district, where they had been relocated in 1989. It is not known whether any charges were brought against the detainees or when they were released. Those who have returned have stated that they did so because conditions at the site were poor and were not what had been promised to them.[16]

- In March 1992, some 150 villagers and activists in Manibeli, Maharashtra were detained during a government operation to relocate residents of the village, which is scheduled for submergence in mid-1992. According to residents, village representatives and NBA activists reportedly first attempted to negotiate an agreement to assist those who wanted to leave so that the police would not have to enter the village. Despite the agreement, a large deployment of uniformed Maharashtran police, plainclothes Gujarati police and Maharashtran government officials entered the village on March 26, ostensibly to provide protection for families they claimed had agreed to be relocated. At about 2:00 p.m., the police surrounded 150 people and told them they were under arrest. They were released at 7:00 p.m.

Early the next morning, bulldozers were brought into the village. Villagers complained that the bulldozers were ruining their fields in violation of a court order blocking the police from damaging the property of those who have refused to leave. At about 10:30 a.m., a group of protesters sat down in the road to block the entry of the bulldozer. The police surrounded the protesters and beat a number of them. Five women were detained until 4:00 p.m. The police also. arrested 55 men who were taken to a school in the town of Rajpipla, some 40 kilometers away, and detained for 12 hours without food. They were then taken to Kevadia, about 16 kilometers from Manibeli. No charges were filed against them, and around midnight they were released and had to walk home.

On March 28, bulldozers damaged the compounds of two families who had refused to leave the village. In protest, the villagers began a sit-down strike. The police lathi-charged the demonstrators, injuring at least ten protesters. The police also reportedly dragged some women from the site by their hair. The police took the camera of one activist who attempted to take photographs of the police breaking up the protest. The camera was returned but the film had been exposed. At least 51 men and

---

[16] Bharat Desai, "Oustees Abandon Alternative Land," *Indian Express* (Bardoda edition), March 4, 1992; Shubha, "The Long March of the Dispossessed," *The Independent*, (Bombay), March 21, 1992.

women were arrested and taken to a temple across the border in Gujarat. Some of the detainees who had been beaten requested medical treatment but were refused. At midnight the group was taken to Kevadia and released. The group proceeded to the Kevadia Colony police station to file a complaint about what had happened. According to an Asia Watch source, when one of the activists attempted to fill out the form, Subinspector Handa told her that she could sign what he wrote or "Get out." The group left without filing the complaint.

Protests continued on March 30, when bulldozers damaged the fields of two Manibeli residents. Since then, a deployment of several hundred police has set up camp in Manibeli. On April 1, the Dhule court issued a stay order on the use of police for further relocation work in Manibeli.

▪ According to NBA activists, during protests in Manibeli on April 11, 20 villagers were arrested, a number of whom were reportedly beaten by police. One suffered a broken nose as a result of the beatings. Strikes and protests continued until April 16, when police surrounded the protesters, injuring at least 33 people, including some children who were later treated for their injuries by doctors in the nearby town of Dhule. Several women alleged that they were sexually molested by the police while being arrested. A woman activist was reportedly dragged from the NBA office and struck on the mouth. Another activist, was reportedly stripped to his underwear and beaten. On April 22, the police dismantled their camp and withdrew from Manibeli. Over the next several days, police officers accompanied by forest officials returned to mark trees for cutting as part of a planned forest clearance before the submergence. When villagers, many of whom depend on the forest for their livelihood, protested and requested a meeting with the forest officials, the police arrested eight leading activists who were ordered into a forestry department truck and driven a short distance from the village. They were then returned to the village and were told that they had not been arrested.

In response to reports of the excessive use of force by the police in Manibeli, the state minister for rehabilitation, Anantrao Thopte, stated before the state legislature that "only after the affected people who wanted to shift asked for police protection were the police sent to the village."[17]

However, a fact-finding mission led by retired Justice H. Suresh of the Maharashtra High Court which visited Manibeli on April 21-22 to look into the recent incidents reached different conclusions. The team found that "the local population had never. any objection to [the former residents] removing any of their belongings." In its report, the team observed that the pattern of arrests by the Maharashtra police presented a "uniform picture":

> The police has [sic] been rounding up a number of persons including women and children, no charges are framed and [they] are later released late at night in Kevadia in Gujarat area. More often than not they [are] not provided any charge-sheet, no tea or food provided and even ladies [are] freed at Kevadia at midnight, against all rules and regulations. The locals have been staging silent protest against uncalled-for outside interference. In return they have been beaten up, their belongings damaged and looted and even women beaten up by male police.

On April 22, the team met with the Additional Collector of the Dhule police, S.S. Gill, about the charges that had been made against the police. Gill reportedly stated that he could not comment because he had not read the reports and that the Supreme Court was the proper place to hear these concerns. To Asia Watch's knowledge, no other investigation of the abuses has taken place.

---

[17]"No Evictions in Manibeli," *Times of India* (Bombay), March 29, 1992.

KENYA

Environmental Heroine or 'Traitor?'

Professor Wangari Muta Maathai of Kenya is one of Africa's most respected environmentalists. She is the founder and director of one of the developing world's most successful grassroots environmental movements. Maathai's organizing and advocacy for the environment has been honored with international recognition and awards, including the Goldman Environmental Prize in 1991. While she has been hailed abroad as a heroine, Maathai was depicted at home as a traitor.

Born in 1940, Maathai earned a master's degree in biology from the University of Pittsburgh. She returned to Kenya to become the first Kenyan woman to receive a Ph.D. at the University of Nairobi and to be the first woman to teach there. Maathai became the head of the University's department of veterinary medicine.

In 1976, Professor Maathai resigned her university position to run for Parliament. When she was disqualified as a candidate on a technicality, Maathai focussed her energies on work in the nongovernmental sector. In 1977, Maathai joined the National Council of Women of Kenya and became a member of its executive committee. Under the auspices of the Council, she decided to strengthen the tree planting efforts which she had already begun from a small nursery in her backyard in Nairobi.

Under the name of the Green Belt Movement, Professor Maathai stimulated the involvement of thousands of Kenyan women in the planting of trees. Her goals were to stop soil erosion, make rural people self-sufficient in fuel wood, foster the survival of native trees and plants, and improve the self-confidence of Kenya women.[1] The Green Belt Movement's 1,500 tree nurseries have employed 50,000 people, 99

---

[1] For a description of the Green Belt Movement see Maathai, *The Green Belt Movement*, (Nairobi: 1988), pp. 17-24.

percent of whom are women.[2] The women, whom Maathai describes as "foresters without diplomas", receive a small payment for every seedling that survives three months.[3] Some of the trees are harvested at maturity for firewood and then replaced with new trees. The Movement has planted and maintained over 10 million trees since its inception, and has some 600,000 members.[4]

Kenya is suffering from both economic troubles and the rapid destruction of natural resources. "Our attitude is to exploit nature," said Professor Maathai. "We use it and exploit it," she said, "but it is clear that in our part of the world, when land is over-exploited and not able to give food, people die."[5]

The Green Belt Movement also works with the National Council of Women of Kenya to teach nutrition with traditional foods and promote family planning. The Movement has been such a success that it has been copied and implemented in twelve other African countries.

Professor Maathai's environmental activism extends beyond the Green Belt Movement. She led the outcry against the destruction of 20 hectares of forest on the outskirts of Nairobi that was destroyed to provide land for the cultivation of roses for export. Maathai countered official claims that the site contained no indigenous trees by presenting

---

[2] In Kenya, as in most of Africa, 80 percent of the farmers and fuel gatherers are women. In the Green Belt Movement, men are not involved in the planting in the nursery, but are involved in the planting of trees on farms. Wangari Maathai, "Foresters Without Diplomas," *Ms.*, March/April 1991, p. 74.

[3] Maathai, "Foresters Without Diplomas," p. 74.

[4] Christopher Boyd, "Kenyan Plants Roots for Reforestation, Political Power," *Chicago Tribune*, January 5, 1992.

[5] Carl Nolte, "Professor Describes the Hazards of Environmentalism in Kenya," *San Francisco Chronicle*, October 1, 1990, p. E6.

a photograph of herself in the cleared forest, clinging to the stump of a recently felled giant hardwood.[6]

Professor Maathai was also a leader in the fight against the construction of a 62-story office tower in the middle of Uhuru Park in Nairobi. The Park is downtown Nairobi's largest green space, the site of many official events and festivities, and one of the few green spaces accessible to Nairobi's slums. The office building would have been the tallest on the African continent and a four-story statue of Kenyan President Daniel arap Moi would have graced the exterior.[7]

Objecting to the construction of the building, Professor Maathai sent letters to Government minsters. When Maathai organized opposition, the Government denied her permission for a public demonstration against the project. She then filed a lawsuit to prevent the proposed project. The suit was dismissed, yet Maathai triumphed as foreign investors withdrew their support of the Uhuru Park complex. "If I didn't react to their interfering with the central park, I may as well not plant another tree," she said. "I cannot condone that kind of activity and call myself an environmentalist."[8]

As a result of her vocal opposition to the proposed 62-story building, she has incurred the lasting enmity of Moi's government.[9] The Green Belt Movement's offices were closed, forcing Professor Maathai to vacate her office of ten years with only twenty-four hours notice.[10] When Maathai filed the lawsuit against the governing party, she was

---

[6] Anastasia Toufexis, "Endangered Species," Time, April 27, 1992, pp. 48-50.

[7] "Kenya, Leaning Tower," *The Economist*, p. 41.

[8] Jane Perlez, "Skyscraper's Foe Draws Daily Scorn," *New York Times*, December 3, 1989.

[9] "How they cut down the tree woman of Kenya," *The Observer*, March 8, 1992, p. 53.

[10] Although the Kenyan Government had not given any financial support, it had provided an office for the use of the Green Belt Movement.

accused of taking President Daniel arap Moi himself to court, a sign of ultimate disrespect.

The Kenyan special police began an investigation into her activities and the government's supporters labeled Maathai and the Green Belt Movement, as "subversive." Such smearing hurt the Movement, which is dependent upon the support of rural women and their communities. "When these people hear second hand that the movement is subversive," Maathai stated, "they don't want to be seen as against the Government, which can lead you into a lot of trouble. And a lot of politicians know that this is the way people feel."[11]

Maathai has been vilified in Parliament. Shortly after Maathai's complaints were made public, parliament interrupted its business to "discuss" Wangari Maathai. Crude jokes were made, members of Parliament have called her behavior "ugly and ominous."[12] Parliament discussion have impertinently centered upon the facts that she is a woman and has been divorced. President Moi declared that she and other opponents to the building "have insects in their heads." Supporters of President Moi have called for a ban of the Green Belt Movement.

Since the Kenyan government last year moved to permit activities by other political parties, Maathai became a leading member of the Forum for the Restoration of Democracy (FORD), a key opposition party.[13]

On January 10, 1992, Professor Maathai took part in a press conference at which members of FORD alleged that President Daniel arap Moi planned a military coup to block the first multiparty elections since 1963.[14] On January 13, after the press conference, over 100

---

[11] Perlez, "Skyscraper's Foe Draws Daily Scorn," *New York Times*.

[12] "Kenya, Leaning Tower," *The Economist*.

[13] Multiparty democracy was legalized in Kenya in December 1991. Until then, the Kenyan African National Union had been the sole legal party.

[14] *Time*, January 27, 1992, p. 39.

policemen swarmed Maathai's home. Maathai was pulled through a window, arrested, and taken to jail. Professor Maathai is facing trial on charges of publishing a "false rumor which is likely to alarm the public."

Maathai was forced to sleep on the floor of a cold cell, without a mattress or blanket, despite her history of arthritis and heart trouble. Her requests to see a doctor were refused. At the time of her hearing the next day, she had to be carried into court on a stretcher. She was hospitalized for nearly two weeks with back trouble after her release.

Professor Maathai believes that after she protested the office building in Uhuru Park, the government was waiting for a chance to arrest her. After her warning of an impending coup, she said, "They felt that this time they had to get me."[15]

Wangari Maathai, along with numerous other women, held a peaceful hunger strike in Uhuru Park to demand the freedom of a number of environmental and political activists in March 1992.[16] On the fifth day of the hunger strike, police attempted to move the women. The police used tear gas and gunfire, but the women refused to leave. The police then attacked the women with clubs. Wangari Maathai was teargassed, clubbed unconscious, and arrested in the same park which she sought to save from an office building. Maathai rejoined the women staging the hunger strike upon her release from the hospital, just days after being beaten unconscious.[17]

News of the police action against the demonstrators evoked an international outcry of concern for Wangari Maathai. The United States Embassy in Nairobi, upon learning of Maathai's earlier arrest on January 10, 1992, expressed their concern to the authorities about Professor

---

[15] "How they cut down the tree woman of Kenya," *The Observer*.

[16] "Maathai beaten unconscious," *Earth Summit Times*, March 9, 1992, p. 1.

[17] Gillian Forrester, "Ex-Pitt Grad Student Stirs Emotion as Activist in Kenya," *Pittsburgh Press*, March 8, 1992.

Maathai's welfare and denial of free speech.[18] The United States Government also voiced in a public statement and in communications with senior Kenyan officials its disapproval of the police action of March 3 against the peaceful demonstrators.[19]

Maathai is facing trial on charges for the "spreading of malicious rumors" from her arrest of January 13, 1992. The trial originally scheduled for May 27, 1992, was postponed and will be reset later this summer. The Kenyan government meanwhile has allowed Maathai to leave Kenya. She is planning to join thousands of other environmental leaders and activists at the Earth Summit this June in Rio de Janeiro.

---

[18] Letter from Martin Cheshes, Director of East African Affairs, Department of State to Jacob Scherr, April 1992.

[19] *Ibid.*

MALAYSIA

An Unholy Alliance of Politics and Logging

The indigenous people who live in the Malaysian rainforest and are dependent on it for every aspect of their ancient culture are now pitted against state and federal authorities, who have a huge financial stake in the forests. Logging and politics are inextricably intertwined; new laws are created to override the old protections. Some, including the conservative International Timber Trade Organization, (ITTO), warn that the whole matter will soon be moot because logging will transform Malaysia's rainforest into a veritable wasteland by the end of this decade.[1] The voracious timber export industry has already caused land erosion, water contamination, the extinction of wildlife and plant species and the annihilation of indigenous cultures, not to mention the wider impact on global warming.

Although most of the profit from logging goes to state officials, the federal government in Kuala Lumpur benefits both economically and, more importantly, politically from logging. By allowing the states to exploit their forests at their own discretion, Malaysian Prime Minister Datuk Seri Dr. Mahathir Mohamad ensures their loyalty to *Barisan Nasional,* the ruling coalition party which he heads. Kuala Lumpur has never had comfortable relations with the two Borneo states (Sabah and Sarawak), so maintaining support from those governments is a political necessity, especially if it is to keep a tight grip on parliament.[2] Mahathir wants Malaysia to be "completely industrialized" by the year 2020.[3]

---

[1] A 1990 ITTO report, cited in "Tropical Heat," *The Economist,* February 15, 1992, warns that Sarawak will have no virgin forest left by 2001.

[2] In Sabah, leaders of the opposition party, Parti Bersatu Sabah, have been detained, and some remain in detention, under the Internal Security Act. For further discussion, see "Malaysia: Detainees in Sabah," *News from Asia Watch,* October 18, 1991.

[3] "Malaysia: The race to 2020," *The Economist,* November 9, 1991.

There is little room in such a plan for indigenous lifestyles, which Mahathir characterizes as "eating monkeys and suffering from all kinds of diseases."[4]

For these reasons, Mahathir has declared an unofficial war against proponents of environmental and indigenous people's protection, who call for a logging moratorium or at minimum a revamping of the existing timber infrastructure. The "war" is waged by repressive legislation prohibiting freedoms of association and assembly; censorship and harassment of domestic and international media; turning a blind eye to corruption and violations of official environmental policies; and the intimidation of environmentalists and indigenous people by means ranging from hired thugs to detention without charge under draconian emergency laws that supersede constitutionally-guaranteed rights.

Malaysian authorities espouse convincing conservationist sympathies but in actuality none of the protective measures is implemented. Asked if there is ever punishment or prosecution for logging practices that violate the ostensibly sound official logging code, such as cutting trees that are too small or cutting too many trees per hectare, one logger answered: "No, there's no prosecution. There's only corruption."[5]

According to a recent article, the scene in the Borneo states of Malaysia is one of rampant waste and destruction.

> It is like open-cast mining: huge bulldozers shift vast amounts of earth and topsoil, which is washed into the river system. Thousands of trees are bulldozed into gullies to form temporary roads. Huge funeral pyres burn with trees deemed too small to send to the coast.
>
> The riverbanks are lined with miles of rotting logs stacked 40-feet high because buyers have rejected them.

---

[4] "Tropical Heat," *The Economist*, 2/15/92.

[5] "Penan's last stand against timber industry pirates," by James Barclay, *Guardian*, January 10, 1992.

They could have been left if the cutters were not inexperienced workers on piece-rates.[6]

A shallow-growing creeper weed eventually greens the devastated land, but the rainforest is not revived.

Mahathir has waged an effective campaign against environmentalists in which their activities are synonymous with sedition and foreigners concerned about Malaysia's rate of logging are discredited as motivated by a racist assumption that non-whites cannot make sound decisions. International environmental activists are condemned as racist "eco-imperialists" and domestic activists are Malaysia's "Number 1 traitors."[7]

The prime minister claims that anti-logging protests are "being used to set up an international infrastructure that can attack and topple the sovereign governments of third-world nations, using the excuse of saving the environment."[8]

Malaysian authorities recently announced the formation of a special task force to be based in Europe, whose US$4 million budget will be financed by the Malaysian Timber Industry Development Council.[9] Its mandate will be to "repel falsehood and lies spread by evil-intended environmentalists," who, officials say, have been "brainwashing the people

---

[6] *Ibid.*

[7] "Eco-imperialists" attributed to Prime Minister Mahathir; "Number 1 traitor" attributed to Sarawak Chief Minister Abdul Taib Mahmud: "Act against 'traitors' call," *Borneo Post*, March 30, 1992.

[8] "Tropical Heat," *The Economist*, February 15, 1992

[9] "Malaysia: Crisis deepens for Dayaks in Sarawak," *Urgent Action Bulliten*, Survival International, April 1992.

of Europe" in order to "damage the country's reputation and image in the western world."[10]

BACKGROUND

Eleven of Malaysia's thirteen states are located on the Malaysian peninsula while Sabah and Sarawak are separated from Kuala Lumpur and the rest of Malaysia by some 200 miles of Borneo Sea. Sabah's rainforest is expected to be "logged out" by 1995.[11] So all eyes turn to Sarawak: its land area is 12.33 million hectares, 38 percent of Malaysia's total land area; in 1990, its logging industry was estimated to generate about $2 billion in foreign exchange, (and logging has only increased since then) and the industry employs some 55,000 persons. But environmentalists and indigenous rights activists warn that the last remains of the ancient Borneo rainforest are being permanently extinguished at a rate three times faster than the Amazon rainforest.

Communal forests, to which indigenous persons have exclusive rights, have been reduced from 30,300 hectares in 1968 to just over 5,000 in 1990. The indigenous people have legal right to the land under the Native Customary Law, but they cannot claim native land rights without applying to the government. The procedure is often expensive, and indigenous people tend not to have currency. In addition, land rights can be overturned through "gazetting" in which state officials print an announcement in the government gazette, which the indigenous people do not receive. If no reply is received within a certain period of time, the land has changed hands.[12] At present, 9.42 million hectares has been gazetted, most of which will be divided into logging concessions.

---

[10] Prime Industries Minister Datuk Seri Dr. Lim Keng Yaik in "Special task force to counter western media propaganda," *Borneo Post*, January 4, 1992.

[11] According to an ITTO report quoted in "Empires of the chainsaws," *The Economist*, August 10, 1991.

[12] "The Children in Empty Huts," by Jeni Kendell, *Index on Censorship*, June/July, 1989.

Indigenous people constitute nearly 50 percent of the state's population. Most of them are entirely dependent on the rainforests for food, medicine and shelter, as well as to maintain their customs and ways of life generally. Deforestation means the extinction of their ancient cultures.

The fight in Sarawak to slow rainforest destruction and protect the indigenous cultures has been fought in two ways. First, there has been a publicity campaign to get domestic and international exposure of the problem, and to combat "misinformation" distributed by officials. Second, the indigenous people have engaged in non-violent protests, primarily in the form of human blockades that obstruct logging roads.

Most of the indigenous people do not read or speak either English or Malay, the main languages of power in Malaysia, and most cannot vote since they are do not hold identification cards.[13] The blockades, therefore, provide just about their only means of empowerment. In the words of one indigenous person, they feel that "[without the blockades] we cannot do anything to stop the company...when we try to defend ourselves, we are condemned as troublemakers."[14]

Among the indigenous people, the Penan ethnic group, an ancient hunter-gatherer society, has been particularly active in blockading timber roads. Their name has become somewhat interchangeable with the movement as a whole. Many Malaysian authorities assert that they are better off changing their 'primitive' lifestyles and becoming incorporated

---

[13] Many people in the interior do not hold identification cards. Sometimes this is the result of not being able to participate in the complicated registration process. In other instances, registration is kept on hold for years, without explanation.

[14] Ulat Ayat, quoted in *The Battle for Sarawak's Forests* by the World Rainforest Movement and Sahabat Alam Malaysia, p. 47.

into the modern world. They say the Penan have been "over-romanticized and over-mythicized by liberal Westerners."[15]

Penan who have been removed from the rainforest (there are only a few hundred now out of some 9,000 Penan who still live in the traditional manner in the forest) reside in government-subsidized "longhouses." There they experience malnutrition, various physical ailments and mental depression. They are not assimilating into modern society, and government efforts on their behalf are reportedly next to nil.[16] Yet success stories appear in the domestic media, claiming that life in the longhouses is a radical improvement for the Penan.[17]

LOGGING AND POLITICAL CORRUPTION

The state has absolute jurisdiction over land matters, a remnant of the enticement package with which the then-called "Malaya Federation" induced Sabah and Sarawak to join the union in 1963. The two states brought additional ethnic diversity to the union as well as a wealth in natural gas and the world's oldest virgin rainforest. To this day, while 95 percent of gas profits go directly to the federal government, (the cause of great federal-state discord), timber concessions and jurisdiction over logging laws are still entirely controlled by the states. The state grants concessions to individuals who then contract out short-term rights to log the land in exchange for a percentage of the profits.

---

[15] "Who are these Penans?" by Ken Yalang, *Sarawak Tribune*, February 29, 1992.

[16] For example, the government sponsors a "flying doctor service," in which a physician is flown into the area (land travel is extremely difficult). There are reports, however, that the doctor comes sporadically and infrequently, and more often than not simply tosses packages of an aspirin-like medicine from his helicopter and spends the rest of his visit shooting at wild game from up in the air. Interviews with Sarawakian representatives, September 24, 1991.

[17] See, for example, "Who are these Penans," by Ken Yalang, *Sarawak Tribune*, February 29, 1992.

Logging continues seven days a week, twenty-four hours a day. At night the forest is lit by giant floodlights. As political offices change hands, so too do the logging contracts. Once a contract is secured, (usually only a one- or two-year arrangement) therefore, literally every minute of its term is utilized in order to make maximum use of the forest's temporary availability. Yet only about 30 percent of the cut trees are used. The rest, often young trees that do not pass export regulations, are left to rot.[18]

Years of unaccountability have yielded a situation in which those who supposedly protect the environment are also the ones who profit most from its exploitation. The situation is epitomized by Sarawak Minister for the Environment and Tourism, Datuk James Wong, saying: "We get too much rain in Sarawak. It stops me from playing golf."[19] Wong, an outspoken proponent of logging, owns 300,000 hectares of forest concessions, and the Limbang Trading Company, one of the nation's largest timber companies. In his own words, "logging is my bread and butter."[20]

Sarawak Chief Minister Abdul Taib Mahmud, who calls anti-logging activists Malaysia's "number one traitors," directly controls 10 percent of Sarawak's logging concessions. He distributes logging licenses, like political favors, at his discretion. Taib's relatives and political allies are said to hold around 1.6 million hectares, roughly one third of Sarawak's timber concessions.[21]

In 1987, the Sarawak state elections were funded almost exclusively by money made from logging. Chief Minister Taib froze

---

[18] "Penan's last stand against timber industry pirates," by James Barclay, *Guardian*, January 1, 1992.

[19] "International experts say Sarawak natives badly affected by logging," *Utusan Konsumer*, March 1988.

[20] *Star*, September 5, 1988.

[21] "In Sarawak, a Clash Over Land and Power," by Raphael Pura, *The Asian Wall Street Journal*, February 7, 1990.

concessions owned by his opponents that covered 1.25 million hectares and which were worth between M$9 billion and M$22.5 billion. Political campaigns are funded with money obtained through logging.[22] Taib says granting concessions to politicians is a good thing because it frees them from their sponsors.[23]

Loggers allegedly falsify records of the species, sizes and origins of cut logs in order to avoid paying higher royalty rates on certain classes of wood. Analysts estimate that 30-40 percent of Sabah's annual logging production is exported with improper documentation.

> [A] shadowy network of businessmen is employing an elaborate system of bribes and kickbacks to document falsely both the species and the volume of the logs being loaded at East Malaysian ports.[24]

An estimated US$100 million in illegal timber is exported, undeclared, by just one of the several groups working illegally in Sabah.[25] Enforcement officials make little impact because their powers are severely curtailed by timber companies' protections and often they "prefer to remain silent in order to share in the secret profits."[26]

Kuala Lumpur espouses sound conservationist practices, while in fact, according to *The Economist*,

> [t]he federal government in Kuala Lumpur and the cliques that control Malaysia's two states in Borneo have a tacit understanding. The states will help generate

---

[22]"The Children of Empty Huts," *Index on Censorship*.

[23]*New Straits Times*, October 4, 1987.

[24]"Cutting down to size," by Doug Tsuruoka, *Far Eastern Economic Review* (*FEER*), July 4, 1991.

[25]*Ibid*.

[26]*Ibid*.

revenue for the federal government from Borneo's natural resources so long as they are left free to run things their own way.[27]

REPRESSIVE LEGISLATION

The Emergency (Public Order and Prevention of Crimes) Ordinance 1969

The Emergency Ordinance grants authorities the ability to detain anyone they suspect of wrongdoing without charges or trial for up to 60 days. Used in the past against gangsters and Communist insurgents, it was most recently directed against Anderson Mutang Urud, from the Kelabit tribe. Mutang Urud is a leader in the blockades and an international spokesperson for the indigenous people. Fluent in Malay, English and Kelabit, he travelled internationally to increase awareness and heighten international concern for the situation in Sarawak. He was instrumental in founding the Sarawak Indigenous People's Alliance (SIPA) in 1991 to disseminate information and campaign against unsustainable logging.

On January 11, 1992, Mutang Urud accompanied Svend Robinson, a member of the Canadian Parliament visiting Malaysia on a fact-finding mission, and Brendan McGivern, a Canadian diplomat, to an anti-logging blockade. Mutang Urud was then detained on February 5 under Section 3 of the Emergency Ordinance, and charged with running an unregistered society, SIPA. (All organizations must be registered with the Registrar of Societies under the Societies Act. Registration can take as little as a month for those that promote the official "party line" and more than three years for groups that go against it.)

Mutang Urud believes that the Svend Robinson affair and SIPA are not the real reasons for his arrest. He points out that the arrest occurred just before the blockade at Long Ajeng, one of the longest-running ever, was to be dismantled by authorities on February 12. As one of the blockade's most prominent leaders, Mutang Urud's arrest would help demoralize the more-than-500 participants and thus make taking it

[27] "The dwindling forest beyond Long San," *The Economist*, August 18, 1990.

apart without complications or resistance that much easier. During detention, Mutang Urud says he was interrogated about, among other things, how best to dismantle the blockade, and was asked to accompany the state and federal agents who did so. (He refused.)[28] Mutang Urud was released on bail on March 3, after protests by Amnesty International and other groups. His trial is set for September, 1992.

Mutang Urud was kept in solitary confinement and interrogated for hours continuously, sometimes until 4 a.m., until he no longer knew whether it was morning or night. For ten days he was held in a cell without a window. He was forced to take cold showers in the middle of the night, to sleep without a shirt, sheets or blankets, and denied medical treatment. Furthermore, his interrogators constantly warned that he might be held under the Public Order provision of the Emergency Ordinance and therefore could be kept in detention indefinitely.[29]

Forests Ordinance

The blockades began over a decade ago but did not draw international media attention until 1987, a year in which 310,000 hectares was logged. In 1985, only 270,000 hectares had been logged. In contrast to the urgent recommendations of the ITTO and other groups, the logging rate has steadily increased. It is estimated that 1992 will see 400,000 hectares cleared -- more if illegal activity is factored into the total.

In immediate response to the international attention attracted by the blockades, the Sarawak Forests Ordinance was amended to make obstructing logging activities or resisting the dismantling of a blockade

---

[28] The blockade at Long Ajeng was clearly considered cause for concern, evidenced by the fact that it was ultimately dismantled by the Federal Reserve Unit (FRU), the toughest group of federal police. A sort of advanced riot police, with special uniforms, they carry tear gas and clubs and have a reputation of being vicious. Earlier blockades were dismantled only by local police and members of the federal Special Branch. Interview with Mutang Urud, April 26, 1992.

[29] Interviews with Mutang Urud, April 10 and April 26, 1992.

a criminal offense punishable by two years in prison or a fine of M$6,000. The amendment also granted forestry officials the power to enlist the assistance of agents of the logging concessions to dismantle blockades. Furthermore, the new law set out that expenses incurred in removing the blockade "must be paid by the so-called offenders to the state government" with interest charged annually until the amount is paid.[30]

Indigenous people and their advocates have maintained that their customary rights to the land are protected by state law, so that any blockades set up on "their" land are therefore not illegal. In 1990, three men from the Kayan community filed an order to stop the felling of trees because it transgressed their native customary land rights as enshrined in the Constitution -- to no avail.[31] Despite these claims, since the amendment was enacted, roughly 500 indigenous people have faced criminal charges under the ordinance. At varying times individuals were denied bail and experienced poor treatment while in detention. (See "Conditions in Detention.") In 1989, eighty Penan, swidden agriculturalists, were held in detention for three months, with the women and children who remained behind facing acute problems getting food. Sarawak Director of Forests Leo Chai explained that the "stubborn" indigenous people needed to be dealt with harshly in order to be "taught a lesson."[32]

Internal Security Act

The Internal Security Act (ISA) allows for the arrest without warrant of anyone considered likely to pose a threat to the security of Malaysia. Those arrested can be detained for 60 days without charge or review, and the Minister of Home Affairs has the authority to extend the detention order for up to two years, renewable indefinitely. Prime Minister Mahathir holds the post of Minister of Home Affairs. Usually

---

[30] *Utusan Konsumer*, May 1988.

[31] SiMBA (Singapore and Malaysian British Association), *Newsletter* May 1990.

[32] Emergency Committee for Human Rights in Malaysia, "Update No. 10: Malaysian ISA Detention and Human Rights Alert," February 16, 1989.

reserved for "religious extremists" and "Communists," the ISA has also been used against environmental activists.

Harrison Ngau, a Sarawak representative of Sahabat Alam Malaysia (SAM) and leader of the anti-logging blockades, was called a "communist stooge" by the government.[33] He was arrested at his office in late 1987 and detained under the ISA for sixty days in the midst of a nationwide series of arrests. He was later released conditionally, prohibited from leaving his home after 10 p.m. and barred from leaving the city of Marudi without a police permit. In July 1987, he had led a group of 12 indigenous people to Kuala Lumpur where they communicated their grievances and remonstrated with the government. The mission yielded no results.

Two other Sarawakians, farmers with the Sarawak Land Development Board, were also detained under the ISA at the same time, although the reasons for this are unclear. Among the hundreds of ISA arrests in 1987, at least 91 were known outspoken critics of the official land policy.[34]

CONDITIONS IN DETENTION

Since 1987, blockade participants who have spent time in jail have described various kinds of inhuman and degrading treatment. These include being kept in shackles and, consequently, being forced to defecate on themselves, and being ridiculed and humiliated for this; receiving inedible food or no food at all; being hit by police; being kept in extremely overcrowded cells without room even to sit or squat; unhygienic conditions (they were given one bucket instead of a toilet for 42 people, and forced to wear the same pair of underwear throughout detention); and being charged excessive bail. In several cases, the indigenous people were not brought directly to the town police station

---

[33] "The dwindling forest beyond Long San," *The Economist*, August 18, 1990.

[34] SOS Sarawak press release.

but to a timber company camp first, where they were slapped around and humiliated.[35]

Those detained under the Emergency Ordinance and the ISA undergo additional forms of mistreatment. Detention is often *incommunicado*; charges are not clarified; legal counsel is not permitted until immediately before the trial.

INTIMIDATION

Timber companies hire toughs to drive their trucks and fill other low-level positions. The men who apply for these jobs tend to be in trouble with the law, and use the forest as a safe haven. They are often heavy drinkers with a history of time in jail. Their appearance is intimidating to the indigenous people, as they tend to be heavily tattooed musclemen who conspicuously carry huge knives known locally "samurais." On three recent occasions, local Sarawakian rivalries turned into bloody fights when the gangsters got involved. One local man had four fingers sliced off when a petty argument escalated.[36]

These gangsters serve as off-the-record disciplinarians. One forestry official, investigating illegal logging areas, was persuaded to give up his inquiry after his wife received a visit at home by two thugs wielding machetes.

The logging vigilantes have terrorized indigenous people with their menacing behavior and by implying that they would gladly engage in headhunting if logging is obstructed. While this may sound unlikely in the west, it has a very real ring to the indigenous people of Borneo, where headhunting among some groups continued until quite recently.

Another means of intimidation employed in Sarawak to silence protest against logging is the practice of unofficial "warnings." Indigenous persons in town for one reason or another run into local police officials,

---

[35] Oral reports and *Utusan Konsumer*, mid-August, 1991.

[36] Interviews with Mutang Urud and others, September 24, 1991, April 10, 24 and 26, 1992.

"by chance." They are "invited" to have a chat in police headquarters or to share a cool drink. They are then warned, "for their own good," to stay away from the blockades, from foreigners, or from environmental activists. These "invitations" are also used as a means of informal interrogation. Indigenous people, intimidated and not wishing to appear ungrateful (for the "invitation"), find it difficult to resist the barrage of questions.[37]

GENERAL HARASSMENT

The court hearings against the indigenous people for obstructing logging activities attracted international attention at the end of 1988. Observers representing different legal groups from various countries flocked to Malaysia and indigenous people traveled three days to attend the hearing. Thereupon, the trial dates were abruptly set back a year. Reasons cited included not being able to get an interpreter (despite having over a year to find one) and unavailability of prosecution witnesses.

> Given that the prosecution have more than a year to prepare their cases and get its witnesses and interpreters, such tactics could only be interpreted as an attempt by the Sarawak authorities to diffuse international protests and avoid embarrassment.[38]

Indigenous people also describe being called to court over and over, only to have their hearings postponed. This is a significant form of

---

[37]Interviews with Mutang Urud and others, September 24, 1991 and April 26, 1992.

[38]Indigenous people arrested in November 1987 and scheduled to be tried in October 1988 had their trials postponed until April 1989. Other trials set for December 1988 were changed to November 1989. Trials set for December 1988 were postponed until January 1990. Emergency Committee for Human Rights in Malaysia, "Update No. 10," February 16, 1989.

harassment as the indigenous people often have to walk days to appear in court.[39]

Court proceedures take place in English, a language not spoken by most indigenous. Court-appointed interpreters translate the proceedings into a language that is similar but considerably more complicated than that spoken by the indigenous people. They therefore are unable to precisely follow the proceedings.

Bruno Manser, a Swiss citizen, lived with the Penan for years during the 1980s. He became heavily involved in the anti-logging campaign and for this reason became *persona non grata* in Malaysia. The government described him as a "subversive Zionist and communist." Logging companies placed a $30,000 reward on his head; Penan were beaten and one was killed in attempts to get information about Manser's whereabouts. Manser was chased by commandos through the jungles. The government established checkpoints and soldiers conducted "sweeps" in the areas where he had reportedly been spotted. His crime: remaining in Malaysia past the expiration of his visa.[40]

In addition to the aforementioned task force to be financed by the Malaysian Timber Industry Development Council in order to counter environmentalists' publicity, *Reuters* reported on April 29, 1992, that Malaysia "may form a special police unit" which would "monitor Western and local environmentalists" who seek to disrupt logging activities.[41]

PRESS CENSORSHIP

Censorship -- both official and unofficial -- is widespread in Malaysia. The British-based *Economist* was banned twice during 1991 for

---

[39] *Ibid.*, and Survival International, *Urgent Action Bulletin*, April 1992.

[40] "The Apostle of Borneo," by Wade Davis, *Outside*, January 1991.

[41] "Malaysian Police May Check on Environmentalists," *Reuters*, April 29, 1992.

articles that looked critically at the Malaysian government, and its distribution was deliberately delayed there three times.[42]

A more common means of reining in the press is a phone call from the Ministry of Information to newspaper editors, warning them to "go easy" on a particular topic. The "advice" is generally heeded because maintaining rapport with government officials is a journalistic necessity.

Few negative reports appear about domestic issues, including logging, primarily because of the high degree of self-censorship. Members of the media are subject to having their works banned, censored or their institutions closed. For example, the political weekly *Mingguan Waktu* was banned in December 1991 on the grounds that it had reported "irresponsibly." Only five months old, it had published criticisms of Mahathir's administration.[43]

Mahathir told members of the Association of Southeast Asian Nations (ASEAN), that Western-style freedom of the press could be a hindrance to developing nations. He said that foreign journalists "fabricate stories to entertain and to make money out of it, without caring about the results of their lying."[44]

He also warned the ASEAN representatives that it is not easy to ban a newspaper or expel a foreign reporter:

---

[42] Delaying distribution serves almost the same function as banning issues yet proves more difficult to censure. The issue is delayed until it is no longer even remotely up-to-date. Readership is therefore substantially reduced, and whatever impact the issue might have had is effectively nullified, while the government avoids the political embarrassment of engaging in outright censorship.

[43] *Attacks on the Press: 1991*, Committee to Protect Journalists (CPJ), March 1992, p. 79.

[44] "Malaysia makes its feelings clear," *IPI Report*, October 1991.

> You don't do such things without getting a bashing from the Fourth Estate and those who consider themselves holier than us."[45]

The *Far Eastern Economic Review* (*FEER*), which just completed an out-of-court settlement in a lawsuit filed against it by Mahathir, had its July 4, 1991 issue banned by the Malaysian government. *FEER*, with a Malaysian circulation of 10,000, was not distributed there because, according to Deputy Home Minister Megat Junid Megat Ayob, the issue contained material which "threatened the security of the nation."[46] The issue in question contained three articles on Malaysia. One described Islamic fundamentalism; another discussed challenges faced by a corporation's new director. The third and by far the most detailed article reports that "illegal logging in both states [Sabah and Sarawak] is rampant and may have foreign connections."[47]

On July 5, 1991, eight foreign environmental activists staged a demonstration in Kuala Baram, a dockyard at the mouth of the Baram River, important for timber export, where logs are floated down from the interior before being loaded into barges and finally onto ships for overseas markets. The next day, two freelance journalists, Frank Momberg of Germany and Anna Leonard of the United States, who were covering the protest from across the river, were detained, interrogated and ultimately deported from Malaysia. According to Momberg, authorities "said I was involved in an action against the security of Sarawak." Leonard confirmed, Malaysian authorities "said we have to leave because 'we have threatened the security of the state.' That's ridiculous."[48]

Neither had participated in the demonstration. They had dispatched stories via fax to international news agencies, including the

---

[45] *Ibid.*

[46] *Attacks on the Press: 1991*, CPJ, p. 78.

[47] "Cutting down to size," *FEER*, July 4, 1991.

[48] Telephone interviews with CPJ.

Associated Press and *Reuters*, and Momberg was writing for *Robin Wood*, a German magazine. Other foreign journalists who had been with them were not detained, presumably because the others were based in Kuala Lumpur, and so were not held under Sarawak state laws.

Today, foreign journalists are prohibited from visiting the indigenous people's "longhouses" and the sites of anti-logging activities. Tourist agencies are required to submit names of all foreigners, tourists and journalists, to the Special Branch for review.

Mahathir explained:

> They [foreign journalists] would be most happy if the country was poor and begged for assistance. But they look for something bad to report if the country is not begging for help...It has become part of their culture to look down upon the coloured.[49]

On February 16, 1992, Rolf Bokemier, editor of the German-based *GEO* magazine and Charles Lindsay, a Canadian photographer, arrived in Sarawak but were not permitted to stay. The two had applied through the Malaysian Tourist Development Corporation in Germany to do a story on tourism in Sarawak but state authorities suspected they were planning an article on the anti-logging campaign.[50] (Bokemier had been one of the first to interview Bruno Manser in the mid-1980s.)

British writer James Barclay was deported from Sarawak and became a "prohibited visitor" in August 1991, after he allegedly filmed a Penan blockade for a Canadian production company. Barclay, author of *A Stroll Through Borneo*, reentered Sarawak after officially changing his name and obtaining a new passport.

He was detained from February 15 through March 17, 1992, under Section 33 of the Immigration Act because of his status as a

---

[49] Mahathir quoted in "Some Foreign Journalists are Jealous of M'sia: Dr. M," *Sabah Times*, September 17, 1991.

[50] *New Straits Times*, March 12, 1992.

prohibited immigrant. He was told, however, that he would be charged with drug trafficking (which carries a mandatory death penalty). He was reportedly kept in poor conditions, denied food and water for two days, and physically abused. During interrogation, his recent *Guardian* article, "Penan's last stand against timber industry pirates," was frequently mentioned.[51]

CONCLUSION

The logging industry is virtually exempt from adhering to the environmentally-sound guidelines set forth by the federal government, because it generates wealth for potential dissident voices in the state governments and thus keeps them loyal to the Malaysian federation. Political bullying and scare techniques enable both the legal and the black market timber companies to engage in logging without restraint.

On paper and in words, Malaysia implements reasonable conservationist practices but in actuality environmental activists and critics of logging are detained, censored and harassed. Through it all, the planet's oldest rainforest, as well as the myriad plant and animal species unique to it are being annihilated, and the fragile human cultures that depend on it are on the brink of extinction.

---

[51] January 10, 1992.

MEXICO

Cutting Through the Haze

Residents of Guadalajara's Reforma district say government officials told them not to worry about a persistent smell of gas only hours before more than 20 city blocks were ripped apart in an explosion on April 22, 1992, that killed more than 200 people.[1] Survivors say they reported smelling gas as early as two days before the explosion, but officials, who investigated the reports, did nothing.[2] The leak, allegedly in a nearby gasoline pipeline operated by the state-owned company Petroleos Mexicanos (PEMEX), may have been detected by Pemex employees as much as a week earlier, but the information only became public as a result of intense media scrutiny in the wake of the tragedy.

The fatal explosion in Guadalajara is a graphic illustration of the costs associated with the abuse of the environment in Mexico. Mexicans have been systematically denied access to information about what kind toxic materials and hazardous wastes are contaminating their environment. Information about potentially devastating development projects such as roads, dams, or power plants, and the right to participate meaningfully in the decision making process regarding environmental risks, is routinely withheld from the citizens of Mexico. Government and industry officials are rarely held accountable for environmental problems and laws protecting the environment often go unenforced. In some cases, those who speak out expose themselves to physical harm or threats, and economic reprisals from the government. In other cases, debate is stifled through a systematic process of government co-optation of environmental advocates. These problems persist in spite of the fact that President Salinas has given a higher priority to environmental and human rights issues.

---

[1]Golden, Tim "Test Was Halted Before Explosion" *New York Times*, April 24, 1992, p. 1.

[2]*Ibid.*

The historic lack of attention to environmental issues has left a legacy of destruction and sometimes deadly health risks in both rural and urban areas. Today, Mexico City is one of the largest and most polluted cities in the world, and other Mexican cities, like Monterrey and Guadalajara, are fast succumbing to similar problems.[3] The population has flocked to the cities and border regions in search of employment, resulting in the creation of whole neighborhoods without sewer systems, potable water or electricity. The factories where the migrants come to work, especially those along the border, were also built before sufficient infrastructure was in place to deal with industrial waste disposal and treatment. The cost of these policies can be seen in increased incidence of lead poisoning among children in Mexico City,[4] rising rates of birth defects and cancer in border towns,[5] and the growing number of deaths and illnesses attributed every year to the smog that hangs over Mexico City. During the most polluted days during the winter dry season, Mexico City schools do not let children play outside, for fear that they will become ill from breathing the smog.

In the rural areas, Mexico's rich natural heritage is at risk. Deforestation is destroying the Lacandon forest, the only rainforest in North America, at a faster rate than the Brazilian Amazon[6], and with it the home of the Lacandon Maya indians. The fate of the Lacandon is duplicated throughout the country as temperate and tropical forests, wetlands, beaches, and deserts are destroyed by roads, logging, agriculture, tourism developments, and oil.

---

[3] "El Defeño, Especie al Borde de la Extinción" ("The Federal District Resident, Species on the Verge of Extinction"), and "Monterrey ya Registra 180 Imeca" ("Monterrey reaches 180 Imeca") *Epoca*, March 30, 1992.

[4] "El Plomo" *La Jornada*, May 27, 1991. (Paid advertisement placed by the Group of 100.)

[5] Cody, Edward, "Expanding Waste Line Along Mexico's Border" *Washington Post*, February 17, 1992, p. 1.

[6] Aridjis, Homero, "Montes Azulez fin de la Lancandonia," *La Jornada*, May 28, 1990.

LACK OF ACCESS TO INFORMATION AND TO PARTICIPATION IN DECISIONMAKING

Average people in Mexico are being exposed to increasing levels of pollutants in the air they breath, the water they drink, and in the food they eat. Until recently, little or no information about types and levels of contaminants was made available to the public; even more rare was the public announcement of possible risk or danger.

Since tunnels carrying waste waters from Mexico City were completed in 1975, agriculture has boomed in the Valley of Mezquital. "Black water" from the outflow pipes has brought to life this once dry region that now provides a large portion of the agricultural products sold in the capital city. The waste waters contain untreated human sewage, and industrial by-products including heavy metals and other highly toxic substances, all of which contaminate the produce grown in the region and eaten by residents of the capital. No information or warnings were issued until a 1990 report by the Agriculture and Water Resources Secretariat (SARH) recommended "major restrictions" on the use of the waste water[7]. To date, no efforts have been made to stop discharges or provide an alternative source of water to farmers in the Mezquital Valley.

Studies have shown levels of lead in produce were twice as high as the maximum allowed by the U.S. Environmental Protection Agency and also exceeded those allowed in Mexico's Federal Health Code[8]. It is estimated that at least 25% of all produce sold in Mexico City is contaminated with heavy metals, yet little effort has been made to alter water use patterns or prevent contamination of rivers and other water agricultural water sources.

The air in Mexico City has been called the most contaminated in the world. Today, residents of the region once famous for its

---

[7]Scott, David Clark "Black Water Makes Valley Bloom" *Christian Science Monitor*; October 10, 1991, p. 12.

[8]*Ibid.*

"transparent" air[9] only rarely get a glimpse of the majestic volcanos and mountains that surround their city. The smog that covers the capital is made up of sulfur dioxide, carbon monoxide, ozone, nitrogen oxide, hydrocarbons and suspended particles, including dust and tons of dried human and animal fecal matter.

Information about the level of contamination, the contents of the smog, the potential health risks, and measures to avoid exposure were not made available to the citizens of Mexico City in a timely manner. Information on pollution levels was often not published until the following day, and data was made public in an averaged form that often had little relationship to the daily peaks in contamination levels.

In March of 1991, Jorge Gonzalez, the leader of the Mexican Green Party, brought a complaint to the newly created National Human Rights Commission (CNDH) claiming that the failure to inform was a human rights violation. In November of 1991, the Commission found in his favor, and issued a recommendation that the Mexico City and Federal Governments should use the mass media, especially radio and television, to inform citizens in a timely manner of the levels of contamination and measures they should take to avoid health risks, and that the raw data on pollutants be made available.[10]

Sergio Reyes Lujan, SEDUE Undersecretary for Ecology, claims that the information requested in Gonzalez's complaint was always available from his office, but nobody was interested until recently. Since the ruling, SEDUE has made some improvements; Reyes Lujan says that

---

[9]Carlos Fuentes, an award winning Mexican novelist, and member of the Mexican environmental group the Group of 100, titled his novel about life in Mexico City, *La Region Mas Transparente* or *Where the Air is Clear*. Before automobiles and industry created the smog that now covers the old Aztec capital, Mexico City was renowned for its clean and healthy air.

[10]Comision Nacional de Derechos Humanos, Recomendacion No. 110/91; November 8, 1991.

he now sends out pollution statistics every hour[11]. New electronic billboards have been placed at strategic intersections throughout the city to provide continuously updated information on contamination levels, which is ironically interspersed with advertisements for cars, one of the primary sources air pollution in Mexico City.

Some activists question the real value of the information provided as a result of the Commission's decision, complaining that raw data is still difficult to come by and that the location of pollution measuring stations skew the results.

The 1988 Mexican environmental law held promise for opening up proposed new projects for environmental scutiny. The law states that any public or private project that creates a potential environmental impact must provide an "environmental impact statement" (EIS) to SEDUE. Based on the EIS, SEDUE either approve or rejects the project, or places binding conditions for approval on the project.[12] Yet according a Mexico City environmental lawyer, since the law was signed in 1988, the "overwhelming majority of public and private entities have never submitted a single EIS."[13]

Even when EISs were completed, environmentalists report that they were routinely denied access to the documents until after a project was approved. Environmental groups challenged the policy of withholding of the studies, claiming the failure to release information in a timely manner rendered the studies useless since concerned citizens could not intervene to expose a faulty EIS. In September 1991, a SEDUE administrative decision, *Associaciones Ecologistas v. Fraccionamiento Punta Farallon*, ruled that the environmental agency must release impact study

---

[11] Interview with Sergio Reyes Lujan, Undersecretary for Ecology, SEDUE, on March 13, 1992.

[12] Articles 28 and 29, Ley General del Equilibrio Ecológico y la Protección al Ambiente, 1988.

[13] Interview with Ambassador Alberto Székely, May 6, 1992.

files before a project is approved.[14] Views among environmentalist about the significance of the ruling are mixed. As one Mexico City environmentalist lamented, "...sure they'll give us the study, 24 hours before the bulldozers move in."

In rural areas, undereducated villagers, accustomed to acquiescing to government demands, are often not informed about the environmental and health risks associated with government programs. For example, in the tropical regions of Oaxaca and Chiapas the Mexican government has been involved in a long term mosquito eradication effort to prevent the spread of malaria. Activists allege that government exterminators armed with DDT inundate villages without warning or permission, spraying homes and dropping bags of the chemical into drinking water wells. According to various witnesses the exterminators themselves, often hired locally, do not use protective equipment while spraying.

Some progress has been made in Mexico in recent years on the issue of public information and participation. While the government's response to the April 22 explosion in Guadalajara can by no means be considered adequate, it showed greater openness than has been the case after previous disasters. PEMEX was identified as the culprit within a week after the accident. But, it remains unclear if the prompt and transparent findings resulted from a government decision to be more open or a result of aggressive press reporting and public outrage.

The government has created commissions to deal with the country's more pressing environmental problems, including Mexico City air pollution and biodiversity protection. Nongovernmental environmental leaders have been appointed to serve on these bodies, perhaps as a signal of greater government willingness to take the issues seriously. But the real impact of these commissions on governmental policy remains to be seen.

CO-OPTING OF ACTIVISTS

The Mexican government has refined an extremely effective system of co-optation of opposition voices, made possible by the

---

[14] *Ibid.*

bureaucracy's presence in practically every sector of society. Co-optation of effective leaders has left the Mexican people with virtually no independent labor unions, indigenous rights organizations, peasant representatives, or free press. Labor unions, for example, are controlled by the government and often issue demands and even stage strikes, yet important issues such as worker safety are subordinated to the government's policy of attracting foreign investors to a cheap and docile labor force. Meanwhile the union bosses, called "charros"[15], make millions from kickbacks.

A number of leading Mexican environmentalists are concerned that debate on critical environmental issues is also being stifled. Many allege that the government attempts to control the environmental debate by co-opting environmental advocates and creating what some Mexican environmentalists have dubbed "eco-charros," or government sponsored environmentalists. Eco-charros claim they speak for the Mexican environmental movement at international forums and at so-called "public hearings" in Mexico, but they represent government-approved rhetoric, not citizen activists. The eco-charros are often better funded than other environmentalists and often receive better coverage from the tightly controlled press.

For example, activists opposing the Laguna Verde nuclear power plant claim that environmental groups allowed to participate in public hearings about the controversial Veracruz plant did not speak to the issues concerning the local citizens, but rather stated the problem in the same terms as the government, thus making way for an easy government response. Advocates also reported that an anti-Chernobyl protest at the Soviet consulate in Mexico City was scheduled to coincide with a large demonstration against Laguna Verde in Veracruz. Laguna Verde opponents claim that the press dutifully covered the small Chernobyl protest while completely ignoring the much larger protest in Veracruz.

Even independent environmental advocates are not immune to pressure from the government. Deals are often cut and silence on one issue is traded for government action on another. The "telefonazo,"

---

[15] A "charro" is a rodeo showman, broncobuster or cowboy. The union charros are said to have tamed labor as the rodeo charro tames the wild horse.

(literally "a blow with a telephone"), a strategic telephone call from high levels of government, often the President himself, is legend in Mexico. Reports of press releases withdrawn or changed, laudatory speeches made, and complimentary opinion pieces appearing in the press after a "telefonazo" are rampant in Mexico City environmental circles. The subtle control over environmental debate allows the government of direct public attention to areas where it is prepared to act and prevent discussion of embarrassing issues.

HARASSMENT OF ENVIRONMENTAL ACTIVISTS

Not all activists can be easily dispatched with a telephone call or a job in the bureaucracy. In some cases, the government, especially local officials, seems to have decided that violence or threats is easier than non-violent co-opting of opposition voices. The Mexican government has a long history of human rights abuses perpetuated against political opponents, including independent labor unions, indigenous rights groups, and outspoken journalists. Especially in the rural southern regions, where federal influence and control are minimal and violence has long been used to solve both political and personal disputes, advocates are at risk.

Fidencio Lopez, Mayor of the small Oaxaca highland town of San Mateo Rio Hondo, spoke out against the powerful landowners and logging interests that were destroying forests surrounding his village. He tried to regain control of the lands and their valuable resources for the impoverished population of Rio Hondo. In early 1992, Fidencio Lopez was shot to death, and the police inspector that accompanied him was seriously wounded. U.S. newspaper reports have linked Lopez's murder to powerful logging interests, whose illegal operations he exposed. The Lopez family reported that federal agents and police have done very little to investigate the shooting of the Mayor and led his widow to believe that she would be required to pay for further investigation.[16]

As in the Lopez case, environmental disputes are often intertwined with economic and political struggles, that have frequently led to violence, especially in remote rural areas. Environmental advocates

[16]Katz, Gregory, "Bitter struggle over forest land tests power of the law in Mexico," *Dallas Morning News*, February 2, 1992.

often are associated with opposition parties, exposing them to additional risk. Frequently, the forces of environmental destruction and the forces charged with upholding the law are one and the same, making the advocate's role extremely difficult, as the following example illustrates.

In 1988, Juventino Gonzalez of Periban, Michoacan organized a group of local citizens to protect the Pico de Tancitaro National Park from illegal logging and agricultural activities, and to educate others about the value of intact forests and a healthy environment. According to Gonzalez, formal complaints about illegal activities have been ignored by local and state officials, who often alert law breakers to the complaints. Gonzalez claims that he has twice been beaten by thugs working for the logging and agricultural interests and has been threatened a number of times by not only by loggers but by people working closely with the mayor of Periban. Gonzalez reports that two fellow environmentalists in the "Committee for the Periban Forest" were jailed after denouncing illegal activity in the park, on charges of "violation of economic rights" of the loggers. According to Gonzalez, the Mayor of Periban, who he alleges is working together with the logging and agricultural interests that are destroying the forest, has picketed the group's meetings and loudly denounces its leaders as liars on occasions when the Committee holds public education meetings. The mayor's actions cause citizens to shy away from the meetings for fear that attendance will subject them to harassment, violence or economic sanctions, said Gonzalez.

Parque Papagayo is the only park in the city of Acapulco, providing a welcome green zone to residents of the city. When a quarter of the park was sold to a developer for a shopping center, opponents complained quietly to authorities. When the new owner cut hundreds of century-old shade trees in December of 1991, the park's advocates made their campaign public and requested the assistance of the Group of 100, a well know Mexico City based environmental group.

After going public the activists reported receiving threats and other forms of harassment from the government. In February of 1992, Dr. Javier Mojica, the leader of the group opposing development on the park land, a young medical doctor, was badly beaten in his home. The two men who beat him also threatened to rape his wife, who was made to watch her husband's beating. Activists allege that the men who beat their companion were members of the Judicial Police force, a body renowned for torture and killings. Police contend that Mojica was beaten by common thieves and have done little to investigate the crime.

Two of Mojica's fellow activists, Carmen Chavez and Ricardo Zermeño, report receiving tax audits that they allege were illegal and intended only as harassment. Some Mexico City environmentalists have also complained about the new "vigilance" of tax auditors.

The beaten doctor had been a leader of the left-wing opposition party, but reportedly renounced his party affiliation to avoid confusing his environmental stance with his political beliefs. It is difficult to say if he was beaten because of his opposition to powerful Acapulco development interests or his opposition political activities. His fellow activists firmly believe that he was targeted because of his stance to protect the park.[17]

Mexico has a long history of violence against the press and, like labor unions and peasant organizations, the press is controlled though pay-offs to underpaid reporters and economic pressure on owners of newspapers and television stations. Honest debate and unbiased reporting are rare in Mexico's mass media. Those who do not report the "truth" according to the government are often threatened or tortured, and in a some cases, killed or "disappeared."

According to opponents of the Laguna Verde nuclear power plant, a Veracruz journalist who reported their points of view on the debate over the plant, received repeated "Mafia style" threats. They report that the journalist received anonymous letters containing photos of him and his family going about their daily business. One photo, for example, was reported to be of the journalist dropping his daughter off at school. The implication in all cases is, the journalist and his family are under surveillance and could be killed or injured at the whim of the anonymous photographer.

To perpetuate the very effective freeze on information, the government must keep employees handling that information from revealing it to the public. "Whistle-blowers" who reveal undesirable

---

[17] Interviews with Alejandro Oscos, (an activist opposing construction of the shopping center) on March 20, 1992 and May 23, 1992.

information to the press often suffer serious consequences. Tijuana's Civil Protection Secretary, Carmen Hernandez de Vazquez, was fired March 13, 1992 after she told reporters that methane gas had collected in the city's sewers and could explode. The day following publication of the an article about the potential danger in the *San Diego Tribune*, Hernandez reports that she was told by an aide to the Tijuana Mayor that they did not like her style of public relations. The aide told her that she had jeopardized the city's tourist trade, one of its main sources of revenue. She was given two days to clean out her desk, she said.[18]

This was not Hernandez's first run-in with the mayor for her openness with the press. Earlier in March 1992, she told reporters that a clandestine dump had been discovered on the outskirts of town. Hernandez presented the city with photographs of the site, which showed several industrial waste drums labeled as hazardous, scattered about the bottom of a deep ravine. Many of the drums had broken open, spilling a green, crystalline substance onto the ground. After reports appeared in local newspapers, the same aide told Hernandez to speak no further about the dump. According to Hernandez, officials preceded to discredit her, calling her an alarmist. After she was fired, a statement was released calling the site a domestic trash dump that contained no industrial waste, she said.[19]

In this case, it should be noted that the local officials with whom Hernandez reports being at loggerheads, were not members of the ruling party, the PRI, but members of one of the country's few opposition local governments. The city of Tijuana and the state of Baja California have a mayor and governor from the conservative National Action Party (PAN).

Even Mexico City-based advocates with international recognition are not free from threats and harassment. Homero Aridjis, an award winning poet and novelist, and founder of one of Mexico's most powerful environmental groups, the Group of 100, reports receiving threats and being continuously harassed. According to Aridjis, he has been excluded

---

[18] Interview with Carmen Hernandez de Vasquez, May 14, 1992.

[19] *Ibid.*

from consideration for government sponsored literary prizes and has had his patriotism questioned on numerous occasions. Aridjis alleges that his phone is tapped and believes that service is cut off when the government wants to prevent his message on a particular topic from being heard. The poet reports having received more than one threat to his life after having taken unpopular stances against the slaughter of dolphins and tropical deforestation.[20]

CONCLUSION

Since taking office in December 1988, President Salinas has made a major efforts to create his international image as an environmental leader. He has been particularly eager to establish his "green" credentials in order to secure a controversial free trade agreement with the United States of America. Salinas has made a number of concrete efforts to improve both the environmental and human rights situations in Mexico. In June of 1990, he created the National Human Rights Commission. In April of 1991, he ordered a pollution crackdown in Mexico City, which resulted in the temporary or permanent closing of over 1,000 factories.

Mexican environmental leaders recognize the efforts of Salinas Administration and report that there have been improvements in openness and government accountability in recent years. Yet they are quick to point out that many of Salinas' actions may be "publicity stunts" to allay environmental concerns in the U.S. about the free trade agreement. Many fear that once the trade agreement is signed, there will be a return to business as usual. There is still a long way to go in Mexico to establish environmental due process and to protect the rights of environmental advocates.

---

[20] Interview with Homero and Betty Aridjis, May 22, 1992. Also reported at April 3-5, 1992 Earth Right Conference, Yale University Law School.

THE PHILIPPINES

A Dangerous Environment for Activists

Environmental advocates and journalists have increasingly become the target of attacks by armed agents of powerful businessmen and politicians in the Philippines. Despite the existence of environmental protection regulations and a constitutional commitment to freedom of expression, protesting against environmental despoliation has proved risky in the past year.

Two individuals were killed by members of the military and militia in 1991 because of their prominent stand against logging. A third, a crusading provincial newspaper editor, was shot and killed in his office shortly after he had published stories and editorials naming local officials in an illegal logging ring, but motivation is still unclear. In several instances between 1989 and 1992, environmentalist activists and local and foreign journalists have reportedly been arrested, threatened or harassed because of their attempts to expose official involvement in violations of environmental laws.

The attacks on environmentalists and environmental journalists as a group are a relatively recent development, reflecting an explosion in Catholic church-backed and internationally funded environmental activism since 1987. The environment has come increasingly into the national spotlight since the late 1980s, when a string of catastrophic typhoons and flash floods swept the country, and remained a key concern in 1991 and early 1992, when the country was alternately battered by both severe flooding and drought.[1] Activists blamed the natural disasters

---

[1]The crisis continues today. A typhoon last November 5 ravaged the central Visayas islands, causing floods which swept across deforested hills and left an estimated 6,000 dead. A month later, 22 provinces on the island of Mindanao were thrown into chaos for six weeks after local hydroelectric power generators were shut down, casualties of dangerously low water levels after years of drought.

on widespread deforestation.[2] The Catholic Bishops Conference of the Philippines endorsed a pastoral letter that, on religious grounds, strongly assailed the despoliation of the Philippine environment and applauded grassroots political action of the type that blocked construction of a nuclear power plant near Manila and a hydroelectric dam in northern Luzon.[3] International aid agencies have encouraged the recent explosion of grassroots environmental action, by channeling funds into the support of locally based environmental projects.

In the battle over rapidly vanishing resources, environmental advocacy has pitted civilians -- including priests, journalists and members of indigenous groups -- against powerful business and political interests with ties to military officials. In Bukidnon province, where logging has been banned since 1989, three priests deputized to arrest illegal loggers have been subjected to death threats, and one, Father Nery Lito Satur, was killed by militia forces involved in an illegal logging ring. Environmental activism in Bukidnon and Palawan has been viewed by some military officials as pro-Communist, a dangerous label in a nation where membership in the Communist Party is a criminal offense, and where suspected members have long been targets of military abuses.[4] In Palawan, members of the largest environmental group, Haribon, were arrested and charged with subversion. The efforts by organized indigenous groups in northern Luzon, Mindanao and Palawan islands to manage the forests in which they have traditionally lived has led to several violent land disputes with absentee concession owners; the killing

---

[2]When the country became independent in 1946, dipterocarp (hardwood species) rainforests covered some 30 million hectares; now, after decades of unregulated logging for export, they stand at about 1 million, according to the Philippine government's own figures.

[3]One international journalist, James Clad, wrote that the document was unprecedented in Catholic Church history. See James Clad, "The fragile forests: church pastoral letter protests against despoliation," *Far Eastern Economic Review*, February 25, 1988, p. 19.

[4]Recent killings of those suspected of ties to the underground movement are detailed in *Bad Blood: Militia abuses in Mindanao, the Philippines*, an Asia Watch report (New York:April 13, 1992) and Amnesty International, *The Philippines: The Killing Goes On* (New York, 1992).

of Henry Dumoldol, an Isneg tribal leader, was blamed on his militant advocacy of tribal management of forest resources in Kalinga-Apayao province.

The involvement of military forces in some of the attacks is particularly troubling. Hundreds of unarmed civilians, including opposition group members, rural peasants, government officials, priests and trade unionists have been killed since Corazon Aquino came to power in February 1986, and with a few exceptions, The risks of opposition are intensified in a situation where police or military forces feel free to commit abuses without fear of punishment.

In 1989, the government responded to the church's campaign with a total ban on timber exports, and a ban on logging for national consumption in 40 of the country's 73 provinces. But enforcement of environmental laws has remained weak. In January, the Justice Secretary admitted that government officials were involved in illegal logging.[5]

ATTACKS ON ENVIRONMENTAL ACTIVISTS

The killing of Father Nery Lito Satur

On October 14, 1991, a priest who had waged an anti-logging campaign from the pulpit was shot and bludgeoned to death. The victim, Father Nery Lito Satur, was one of 46 parish priests in the province deputized as official forest guards. In the weeks leading up to the killing, Satur had confiscated lumber worth some 40,000 pisos ($1,600) in his parish of Guinoyoran, and had spoken out against illegal loggers. Satur was killed on a Sunday, minutes after he had left a remote village of Guinoyoran after saying mass. In signed affidavits, two witnesses to the crime said three men, two of them masked, jumped in the path of Satur's motorcycle, pumping five bullets into his body and finishing him off by crushing his skull with a rifle butt.[6]

---

[5] "DOJ [Department of Justice] confirms government men into illegal logging," *Philippine Daily Globe*, January 24, 1992.

[6] See *Bad Blood: Militia Abuses in the Philippines*, (Asia Watch, New York: April 1992) pp. 36-39.

Witnesses and other credible sources interviewed by Human Rights Watch identified an army intelligence officer and five members of the local militia as the perpetrators.[7] The group was involved in an illegal logging activities which Satur publicly challenged. Two of the suspects testified in court that Satur was killed because he was a threat to illegal logging rings. A court trial is currently underway against four suspects.

According to Malaybalay Bishop Guadencio Rosales, the church has withdrawn its priests from Guinoyoran because it judges the risk too great there.

Two other priests active against illegal logging, Father Cirilo "Loloy" Sajelon of Valencia and Father Rino Bargola of San Jose, have received several death threats in recent months. Priests and media reports both suggested that soldiers, CAFGU and prominent local businessmen were involved in the illegal logging rings.[8] In order to protect themselves, the priests in early 1992 traveled with local police officers or parishioners, saying they feared going out alone.

---

[7]Two of the suspects, Guillermo G. Ipanag and Carlito Baraquil, both members of the Citizen Armed Force -- Geographical Unit militia forces, gave testimony in the Municipal Trial Court of Valencia, Bukidnon against four other suspects in an October 1991 preliminary hearing for murder. They named the "mastermind" of the killing as Sgt. Catalino Gabison, and the triggermen as Datu Bantu Domia, Allan Cesar Abesta and Crispin Onor, all members of an armed religious cult.

[8]Carol O. Arguillas, "Log Ban Advocates Called Subversives," *Philippine Daily Inquirer*, October 19, 1991.

The Killing of Henry Domoldol

Henry Domoldol, head of a community association involved in the struggle to keep forests under tribal management, was shot dead on July 26, 1991 as he was coming out of his home in the village of Kopis in the northern province in Kalinga-Apayao. According to witnesses, including two of his sons, the gunmen were members of the Philippine Army and paramilitary organization, the Civilian Armed Forces Geographical Units. After pumping his body with bullets, Domoldol's assailants cut a finger off the corpse and took it away with them.

Domoldol, 55, a member of the Isneg tribe, founded the Nabuangan Community Alliance, an association of five tribal villages. He was widely known for his promotion of the community's right to manage its own forest resources, and had been negotiating with the national government to promote the community-based program. The Alliance was working in coordination with the Friends of the Earth, a U.S.-based international environmental organization, and a Manila-based legal aid association for indigenous groups, the Legal Rights and Natural Resource Center.

For centuries, the forestland of Kalinga-Apayao has been home to tribal groups who generally have no formal title to the lands. The same forests harbor members of the armed wing of the banned Communist party, the New People's Army. The military has been engaging in heavy bombing and "clearing" operations against insurgents in the province for the past several months. The conflict has led to political polarization, and local community organizations have not escaped suspicion. Domoldol's organization had been labelled as "Communist-infiltrated" by military officials. According to friends and family members, threats and assassination attempts against Domoldol predated present military operations.

Local Isneg leaders look at the conflict differently, however. They claim that the military is working in coordination with logging companies in order to open up the rich Isneg dipterocarp forests for logging. While the motive of the killing remains difficult to assess, similar operations in Mindanao in the 1980s which forced the evacuation of tribal groups paved the way for sale of land to logging concessions.

Arrests and Threats Against Environmental Activists in Palawan

On the remote westernmost island of Palawan, a region with the largest remaining stands of virgin forest, several incidents of arbitrary arrests and threats have occurred since 1989. In 1989, stories describing the destruction of the rainforest and fishing grounds there and implicating politicians in the plunder began to surface in the press and in international environmental circles. The victims have primarily been members of Haribon, the largest nongovernmental environmental organization in the Philippines, or their community contacts from the local indigenous communities. But members of official environmental agencies have also been targeted in some cases. A government marine preservation director stationed in Palawan who is well-known for her vigilance against dynamite and cyanide fishing -- both illegal in the country -- reported being threatened "many times."[9]

There have been allegations of official involvement in logging and smuggling at the highest levels. In October, 1990, an environmental committee of the Provincial Board had recommended the investigation of Palawan's Government Victoriano Rodriguez and Provincial Engineer Ricardo Gadiano for a foiled smuggling operation involving illegally cut lumber.[10] Media reports have said that Speaker Ramon Mitra, a Palawan congressman and former Presidential candidate, receives logistical and financial support for his campaigns from the island's richest logger, Jose Alvarez.

Arrests of Haribon Members

In 1988, Haribon began a campaign to save the remaining rainforests of Palawan, much of which is licensed out to logging concessionaires. The official reaction to Haribon's campaign was adversarial, according to Haribon officials interviewed by Human Rights Watch. On February 12, 1991, nine members and officers of Haribon were arrested at their homes and interrogated by the Philippine National

---

[9] Barbara Goldoftas, "Environment: Green Activism a Dangerous Calling in the Philippines," *InterPress Service*, December 4, 1991.

[10] "Palawan board bares lumber smuggling try," *Daily Globe*, October 9, 1990.

Police. Later, 5 more Haribon members were arrested and charged with subversion (membership in the illegal Communist Party of the Philippines) after Haribon members returned from an investigation of a report by their local contacts, Palawan tribal leaders, that they had found a large cache of illegal logs next to a military encampment. In a province with no historical presence of Communist rebel forces, the highest military official in Palawan, Brig. Gen. Braulio Balbas of the Western Command, said Haribon "is pretending to be a militant environmental organization but is actually a front of the Communist movement." He told reporters that 14 of these Haribon members "admitted" to having links with the Communist Party, based on "intense interrogation."[11] Haribon denied the charges, filed counteraffidavits and said the warrantless arrest "was designed to silence them in their campaign for environmental conservation...and particularly in the monitoring/reporting of logging activities in Palawan involving the military." Congressman Mitra had earlier also made allegations that the group had ties to the Communist Party. The trial was ongoing in early 1992. The military filed rebellion charges against attorney who represented the group, human rights lawyer Joselito Alisuag, on December 3, 1991 based on the "confession" of a surrendered rebel. Alisuag denied all the charges, and the case was still being investigated by the Provincial Fiscal's Office in early 1992.

A HAZARDOUS CLIMATE FOR JOURNALISM

Formal censorship ended with the fall of President Ferdinand Marcos and the accession of Corazon Aquino to power in 1986. Paradoxically, while reporters are now free to write about controversial issues, they are now exposed to greater physical danger than under Marcos. According to the Committee to Protect Journalists, 32 journalists have been killed under the six years of Aquino--as many as were killed during the entire 14 years of the Marcos dictatorship. Human Rights Watch believes that at least twice that number may have been beaten, attacked or threatened. Few suspects have been apprehended in the

---

[11] Owen Masaganda, "16 Rebel leaders nabbed in Palawan," *Manila Bulletin*, Monday, March 11, 1991, p.1; Juliet M. Labog, 'Balbas: Haribon staff arrested in Palawan are rebs," *Philippine Daily Inquirer*, February 23, 1991, p. 13.

journalists' killings, and no suspect had been convicted at the end of 1991.[12]

Journalists investigating illegal logging or mining have reported frequent instances of death threats and harassment, but in few cases has this served to silence them.

Environmental reporting "is not about pollution, it's about power," explained Marites D. Vitug, a journalist who received death threats following November 1989 publication of her article, *Money Grows on Trees*, describing the destruction of the rainforest in Palawan. In a country where the business and political elite are indistinguishable, and where elections are generally won by the biggest spenders, political fortunes have depended almost exclusively on profits from logging, mining and cash-crop plantation farming. Forest concessions are owned by a small business elite which includes family members of several of the most powerful politicians in the country. Media reports have backed up activists' claims that concession owners have continued to log restricted forests in violation of environmental restrictions, and that illegal logging has been assisted by members of the military, police and even corrupt officials/forest guards of the agency responsible for preserving forests, the Department of Environment and Natural Resources (DENR).

Journalists say business and political leaders have also increasingly used criminal libel charges with astronomical punitive damages in the attempt to silence journalists and their publishers. Reporters exposing the involvement of the rich in destruction of the environment have also been the target of punitive lawsuits.

Press freedom advocates say the constant threat of libel suits has bred restraint in publishers and television networks. In the Philippines, libel may be a criminal charge, carrying with it the threat of imprisonment as well as fines. Once an indictment of libel has been handed down, Philippine courts must issue an arrest warrant, and defendants are released only after posting bond.

---

[12] "Media Deaths 1986 to August 1991," *Philippine Journalism Review*, Vol. 2, No. 2, September 1991, p. 21.

Killing of Nesino Toling

One journalist, Nesino Paulin Toling, editor of a the *Panguil Bay Monitor*, was shot and killed while he was along in his tiny, two-desk office typing a story on April 14, 1991.

At about sunset, a man walked into Toling's office and fired five shots into his head. Police have arrested a security guard but say he was a paid killer.[13] They have advised other journalists to carry guns. Toling's widow, who continues to publish the 3,500-circulation weekly, keeps a .38-caliber pistol in her desk.

Human Rights Watch believes he was killed because of his articles exposing corruption. Among other controversial stories, Toling accused a general of protecting illegal loggers.

Editors have tried to discourage reprisal killings by publicizing threats to their reporters. But the threat remains in a society where hundreds of political warlords control private armies, and the police charged with responsibility for public security are themselves implicated in killings, extortion and kidnapping rings.

Threats Against Journalists Investigating Environmental Issues

The telephoned death threat against Marites Vitug came one day after a popular national daily, *The Manila Chronicle*, had published her story on the destruction of rainforests in Palawan, "Money Grows on Trees." Vitug, a 1987 Nieman Fellow who has written for *New York Newsday*, *The Christian Science Monitor*, and *The New York Times*, faces a 26-million peso ($1 million) criminal libel suit filed by Jose "Pepito" Alvarez, the owner of much of Palawan's forest concessions. Her co-author in a similar article published later in *The Far Eastern Economic Review*, James Clad, also told Human Rights Watch that he received a death threat by phone.

---

[13] Bob Drogin, "A Deadly Beat for Journalists," *Los Angeles Times*, July 14, 1991.

In 1991 and early 1992, at least seven others who reported on local officials' involvement in illegal logging or mining were threatened. American human rights activist Kerry Kennedy Cuomo, broadcast journalist Judith Moses and two Philippine journalists, Marites Vitug and Howie G. Severino, were forced to hide and leave the island early after a group of men, at least one of them armed and several identified as military and police officials, appeared at their hotel on February 28, 1992. Cuomo and Moses were filming a story on logging practices for TBS' "Network Earth." Among other things, they interviewed families of six young men, all members of the local indigenous tribe, murdered by logging concession guards working for the Pagdanan Timber and Nationwide Princesa Timber Co., both owned by Jose Alvarez.

On the way back to their hotel that evening, a policeman hitched a ride and later told them he would accompany them to their hotel. At the hotel, a group of about eight men had checked in, and had evidently been asking questions about their visit all day long. One of the men pulled aside his jacket to flash a pistol at Moses. Another was identified as the National Bureau of Investigations chief for Palawan, while still others were identified as Western Command army officers moonlighting for the Pagdanan Timber Co. The NBI official questioned the group's porters and driver in the presence of the news team. All were wearing civilian clothing and had been drinking for several hours.

Joey R. B. Lozano, a journalist in the province of South Cotabato, received threats after he broke a story about how mining was devastating the environment in tribal reserves, forcing him to leave town temporarily. Lozano, editor of the *Ecology Advocate*, an ecology-oriented newspaper published in an unlikely outback community in southern Mindanao, nearly lost his life to an assassin's bullet five years ago after writing about another controversial topic. "My strategy is simple," he said. "Write, and hide."

A "CHILLING" EFFECT OF LIBEL

Reporters have also been burdened by multiple libel charges. The phenomenon may a predictable result of the excesses of an overly rambunctious post-censorship press -- a press where, in Manila alone, 20 newspapers vie for readership with juicy political tidbits and titillating headlines. But increasingly, journalists say, charges are filed by those in power expressly to stop journalists from pursuing stories which hurt their interests. Most journalists with two or more years of experience face at least one libel charge.

After Marites Vitug received the death threat, the subject of her story, Jose Alvarez, charged Vitug with criminal libel and sued for 25 million pesos ($1,000,000) in damages. (A Manila journalist's salary averages about 60,000 pesos a year). Mitra's lawyer threatened to do the same. Three and a half years after charges were originally filed, the case remained unresolved. If Vitug loses the criminal charge against her, she may go to jail.

CONCLUSION

The effect of libel and threats has been to discourage some journalists from taking risks. "The chilling effect of a libel suit is real," said Vitug. "It serves as a constant reminder not to tread on dangerous ground." In one known case, a journalist who wrote an exposé on illegal logging left the country following death threats. News analysts say others have been discouraged by their publishers, particularly publishers of provincial or rural newspapers, which are more vulnerable than city papers to economic collapse in the event of costly libel suits. Journalists who take risks are "out on a limb," operating without the institutional structures that may protect them against legal or violent retaliation. In contrast, the Catholic Church and the various international environmental networks continue to provide at least a marginal sense of protection for environmental activists. The killing of the environmentalist priest in Bukidnon, for example, led the parish communities to "circle the wagons" around their parish priests, and to an international campaign pressuring the government to find the perpetrators. The continued proliferation of private armies and poorly paid militia, however, means that no activist is genuinely secure from acts of officially sanctioned violence.

THE FORMER SOVIET UNION

A Poisonous Legacy

The socialist state envisioned by Karl Marx and Vladimir Lenin was to be a society that would affirm the fundamental equality of human beings, meet their material needs, protect their rights, and ensure the rational and efficient use of natural resources. The quest for that utopia was cloaked in almost total secrecy and deception, and has led to environmental destruction and degradation on an unprecedented scale:

- 70 million out of 190 million Soviets living in 103 cities breathe air that carries five and more times the allowed limit of pollutants.

- Steel mills still use antiquated open-hearth technology and belch out tons of industrial wastes and toxic chemicals every year. In many industrial cities infant mortality is rising, while the average life expectancy for Soviet men is down to the level of average life expectancy in Paraguay.[1]

- Out of 1.5 billion acres of cultivated land in the Soviet Union, by 1989 nearly half was imperiled by overcultivation, pesticide contamination, or flooding from mismanaged irrigation.

- An estimated 130 nuclear explosions have been conducted for "peaceful purposes" -- geophysical investigations, to create pressure in oil and gas fields, or to move earth -- resulting in untold contamination of land, water, and people.

---

[1] Murray Feshbach and Alfred Friendly, Jr., *Ecocide in the USSR*, Basic Books, 1992, p. 4.

- The Aral Sea, once larger than Lake Huron, has shrunk in volume by two-thirds as a result of a drive to raise Central Asia's cotton output through irrigation. Wind carries toxic salts from the sea's exposed bed to fields. The chemicals then wash into the drinking water supply.

- A 1957 explosion at the Kyshtym nuclear weapons production plant left hundreds of square miles of land contaminated with radiation.

- A chemical plant accident in the Ural Mountain city of Ufa in 1989 released phenol into the drinking water supply. More than 400 people were treated for phenol poisoning.

Throughout its 70-year history, the Soviet Union repeatedly proclaimed its efforts to protect public health and environment. The official line was that the Soviet state, led by the infallible Communist Party, was capable of incorporating the interests of all people into all of its policies. Early central economic programs included ambitious plans to improve public health and protect nature. Emissions standards for water, air and soil were among the strictest in the world. There was even the appearance of some environmental debate. The government widely publicized its decision to abandon a plan to divert water from several north-flowing Siberian rivers to irrigate land in Southern Russia and Central Asia in the face of public opposition. The Soviet Union was an active participant in international environmental agreements, institutions, and conferences.

At home, the Soviet government suppressed any meaningful discussion of environmental issues. In 1947, a law was passed which prohibited publication of all economic and social data.[2] It was not until the death of Joseph Stalin that the first postwar statistical handbook was issued. Even then, much of its contents was falsified. According to Murray Feshbach and Alfred Friendly, authors of *Ecocide in the USSR* -- the first definitive work on Soviet health and environment -- from 1975 to 1986 Soviet health officials knowingly concealed and even altered the official

[2]The State Secrets Act of 1947.

tally of infant mortality.[3] Data which did not support the myth that conditions in the Soviet Union were always improving were deliberately destroyed or changed.

As Leonid Kruglov, an environmental journalist, wrote in the newspaper "Selskaya Zhizn," "That is how we lived, not knowing what kind of gases we were breathing, what kind of liquids we were drinking, how great the pesticide level was in the meager food products we won after battling the waiting lines. All this information was gathered and stamped 'For Official Use' and hidden away."[4]

Environmental debate in the former Soviet Union was restricted through censorship and control of the mass media. Under Communism, all forms of mass media were owned and controlled by the Party, which allowed only the publication of material that supported its interests. The Party's censorship arm, Glavlit, annually compiled lists of topics that could not be discussed in the Soviet press. When an oil pipeline burst and spilled hundreds of cubic meters of fuel into the Sukhona River, killing everything it came into contact with, local newspapers, under the watchful eye of Glavlit, only reported: "At the location of the accident there was partial pollution of an insignificant section of one of the rivers."[5]

Until last year, the Soviet Constitution also guaranteed the Communist Party a virtual monopoly on public association. Under the threat of arrest, public organizations were forced to disband or go underground. The Party also coerced people, sometimes brutally, into silence on issues that ran counter to the government's interests.

For example, the founder of the Moscow Trust Group, an anti-nuclear organization which was founded in 1982, suffered forced psychiatric detention and constant police harassment before his

---

[3] Feshbach and Friendly, *Ecocide in the USSR*, p. 206.

[4] "Ecological Notebook: There is No Other Choice," *Selskaya Zhizn*, Moscow, February 13, 1992.

[5] *Ibid.*

emigration to the U.S. in 1983.[6] A provincial court commission used the Group's founding statement to condemn a member to a labor camp sentence in 1982. Five more of the group's members were later sent into exile.[7] In addition to formal trials and sentences, activists were harassed in a variety of ways -- their phones disconnected, their mail confiscated, and their apartments bugged.

In 1986, Piotr Kozhevnikov was working for the government water inspection agency, which is charged with controlling water pollution, on a ship in the Gulf of Finland. He discovered, ironically, that the ship was itself illegally dumping oil and sludge into the Gulf. After repeated attempts to bring this activity to the attention of higher authorities, he was transferred from his job. He was later harassed and ultimately arrested for "crimes against the state," including espionage, extremism, and anti-Sovietism. He was placed in a psychiatric ward for ten months, stood trial, and was released only after extended public outcry against the handling of his case.[8]

The Communist government not only silenced the voices of individuals and dissident groups but also took steps to ensure the relative passivity of its people. Factories and military installations poisoned workers with polluting technology while serving as the sole providers of housing, food, and recreation, creating a system in which the citizenry was utterly dependent on the state. The government promised citizens higher salaries and special privileges to go to work in industrial cities such as Nikel, where a giant metal works has left the land barren for a twenty miles around, and then restricted them from moving elsewhere. Even if workers could move, there were few places to go where the quality of life or environmental conditions would be any better.

In a nation obsessed with national security and secrecy, it is not surprising that the military-industrial complex turned out to be a major

---

[6] "From Below: Independent Peace and Environmental Movements in Eastern Europe and the USSR," *Helsinki Watch*, October 1987, p. 108.

[7] *Ibid.*, p. 112.

[8] "Delta," Report by Ecologia, Harford, Pennsylvania.

contributor to environmental degradation in the former Soviet Union. Much of the forced industrialization during the early part of the century was undertaken to meet wartime demand. Whole industries were thus immune from environmental control. During World War II, more than 1,700 large enterprises were packed up and moved into western Siberia, with severe consequences for the environment. Writes Kruglov, "The people were winning a victory over fascism and there was no time to observe any ecological norms."[9]

The Soviet nuclear weapons program was also developed in complete secrecy and outside environmental restrictions. The development and production of nuclear weapons took place in "closed cities," many of which never even appeared on Soviet maps. Between 1949 and 1963, more than 300 nuclear tests were conducted at the Semipalatinsk test site in Kazakhstan, most of them above ground.[10] The military usually evacuated residents -- with little or no warning or explanation -- before the tests, but many have spoken of witnessing the blinding flashes and mushroom clouds. The effect of the tests on local health conditions is impossible to judge because the government would not reveal health statistics for the region.[11]

Just three years ago, officials finally acknowledged two terrible accidents at nuclear weapons production facilities. It was revealed that in 1957, 70 to 80 tons of radioactive material in a nuclear waste storage tank at the secret Kyshtym site exploded, contaminating hundreds of square miles around the zone.[12] In the year following the accident, nearly 11,000 people were evacuated from the zone. While officials claimed no significant health effects had been detected in the population,

---

[9] "Ecological Notebook," *Selskaya Zhizn*.

[10] The Limited Test Ban Treaty of 1963 banned nuclear tests in the atmosphere, oceans, and space.

[11] D.J. Peterson, "The Impact of the Environmental Movement on the Soviet Military," Radio Liberty/Radio Free Europe Report on the USSR, March 15, 1991.

[12] Thomas B. Cochran and Robert Standish Norris, "Soviet Nuclear Warhead Production," February, 1991, pp. 21-26.

survivors told of numerous instances of cancer among the victims of the accident. The government has also recently acknowledged that beginning in 1951, the Mayak weapons production plant near the city of Chelyabinsk pumped vast amounts of radioactive waste -- billions of curies -- into Lake Karachay. Radiation levels around the lake were still high enough in 1990 "to provide a lethal dose" in sixty minutes of exposure.[13]

The Chernobyl accident in 1986 represents a major turning point in Soviet history. It was the first major test of glasnost. The accident was not officially announced until three days after it occurred, and then only under intense international pressure. In June, the Ministry of Public Health issued a directive that read in part: "4. Information about the accident is to be kept classified....8. Information about the results of medical treatment is to be kept classified. 9. Information about the extent of radioactive injuries suffered by personnel who took part in the elimination of the consequences of the accident is to be kept classified."[14] It took three more years for the first detailed, though still incomplete, report on the scope and intensity of the accident to be released.

Chernobyl accelerated the opening up of Soviet society. Reports of previous industrial accidents and previously banned writings began to appear. A law on freedom of the press was passed in July, 1990, and legislation legalizing public associations, including political parties, was adopted in October of that same year.

With more openness came growing environmental activism throughout the country. Hundreds of new environmental organizations were formed, environmental newspapers and journals began to appear, and protest demonstrations and rallies were held. In 1989, over 1000 enterprises were forced to either close or scale back production at least temporarily for environmental reasons. Dozens of nuclear power projects were abandoned. Public opposition also stopped other electric power projects, including Moscow's huge gas-fired Severnaya plant and several

---

[13] *Ibid.*, p. 20.

[14] Feshbach and Friendly, *Ecocide in the USSR*, p. 152.

ill-conceived hydroelectic plants.[15] Under pressure from the environmental lobby in Kazakhstan, nuclear testing was halted at the Semipalatinsk test site.

Since August 1991, Russia has adopted comprehensive environmental protection legislation giving citizens greater enforcement rights and access to the courts, as well as a law requiring environmental impact assessments. An interrepublic agreement on the environment signed in February acknowledges "the right of each individual to a natural environment favorable to life and ecological safety...and a responsibility before our peoples, the peoples of other countries, and future generations for ensuring conditions for life and well-being."[16] The Russian Ministry of Ecology and Natural Resources has a prepared a report for the Earth Summit in Rio de Janeiro which presents new and honest information about the environmental legacy of Communism. "After many years of reading everything having to do with ecology between the lines, the information presented at the Rio conference seems like a confession," comments journalist Kruglov.[17]

In spite of the advances of recent years, the former Soviet Union has a long way to go towards reversing its legacy of deception and destruction. Efforts to accurately assess the environmental and health situation are still hampered by government control over data, the lack of modern equipment to monitor and analyze environmental conditions, and the scarcity of funding for comprehensive studies. Just in February, nongovernmental organizations meeting at Tomsk, a nuclear weapons production facility, complained that the government was still withholding information about the impact of activities at such facilities from affected

---

[15] D.J. Peterson, "Hard Times for the Environment," Report on the USSR, RFE/RL, November 15, 1991.

[16] *Tass News Service*, Moscow, February 9, 1992.

[17] "Ecological Notebook," *Selskaya Zhizn*.

populations. Their joint statement declared, "It is completely inconsistent with basic human rights."[18]

The court system is in disarray and is ill-equipped to deal with unfamiliar cases of environmental law. The budget for the Russian Ministry of Ecology and Natural Resources, the environmental enforcement agency, has been cut 50 percent for 1992, leaving it with few resources to carry out even its limited powers. Hundreds of orders to shutdown polluting enterprises have been reversed. As Svet Zabelin of President Yeltsin's Environmental Policy Council points out: "Sausage is first in people's minds. It is human nature in hard times."

The environmental challenges that the former Soviet Union faces are enormous. The restoration of its environmental health will take years. However, with the efforts to establish public accountability and public participation, there is hope.

---

[18] "Socio-Ecological Consequences of Nuclear Military Production and Nuclear Weapons Testing on the Territory of the former republics of the Soviet Union," Tomsk, February 1992.

THE UNITED STATES OF AMERICA

Punishing Nuclear Whistleblowers

THE NUCLEAR WEAPONS INDUSTRY

Nuclear weapons production is one of the largest and most dangerous industries in the United States.[1] The U.S. Government has produced over 60,000 nuclear warheads since the 1940's,[2] and maintains a vast complex of laboratories, processing and production facilities, and test sites employing over 100,000 people and occupying 3,350 square miles of federal land in 13 states[3] at an annual cost of nearly $2 billion dollars.[4] Private corporations and universities operate the complex under contract to the U.S. Department of Energy (DOE).

Over the last fifty years, the industry has released vast amounts of hazardous chemicals and radionuclides into the environment,[5] and is plagued by scores of dangerous production plants and hundreds of

---

[1] D. Reicher and S. J. Scherr, *Hidden Dangers: Environmental Consequences of Preparing for War*, p. 35 (1990).

[2] T. Cochran, W. Arkin, R. Norris & M. Hoenig, *Nuclear Weapons Databook*, p. 2 (1987).

[3] Office of Technology Assessment, *Complex Cleanup: The Environmental Legacy of Nuclear Weapons Production*, OTA-0-484, p. 15 (1991).

[4] The Department of Energy is requesting $1.9 billion dollars for its 1993 nuclear weapons production and research activities. See, Gray, *Facing Reality: The Future of the U.S. Nuclear Weapons Complex*, p. 7 (The Tides Foundation, May 1992).

[5] See, United States Congress, Office of Technology Assessment, *Complex Cleanup: the Environmental Legacy of Nuclear Weapons Production*, OTA-O-484 (February 1991).

leaking toxic and radioactive waste dumps,[6] as illustrated by the following examples.

In Eastern Washington, the Hanford Nuclear Reservation has discharged more than 200 billion gallons of liquid radioactive and chemical wastes into unlined ponds and trenches contaminating over 100 square miles of groundwater. Tanks filled with highly radioactive liquid wastes have leaked more than 200 kilograms of toxic plutonium into the ground, which is enough for nearly 50 Nagasaki-sized bombs.[7]

In 1990, after a three-year, $1 billion dollar renovation,[8] DOE's K Reactor at the Savannah River Site in South Carolina discharged thousands of curies of radioactively-contaminated cooling water containing tritium into the Savannah River.[9] A number of drinking water plants, food processors, and oyster beds on the Savannah River had to be shut down until the tritium concentrations had diminished. This spill followed dozens of other releases at the site over the past eight years.[10]

The Idaho National Engineering Laboratory dumped nearly 1,000 pounds of plutonium, more than 200 pounds of uranium, and 90,000 gallons of organic solvents into shallow trenches. These and other laboratory's hazardous wastes have seeped into the Snake River Aquifer, a vital water source in the Northwestern United States. From 1957 to

---

[6] Reicher and Scherr, p. 35.

[7] *Ibid.*, p. 36.

[8] DOE, Congressional Budget Request, DOE/CR-0001, February 1991.

[9] Watkins, James D., Secretary of Energy, Press Conference Transcript; Augusta Sheraton, Augusta, Georgia, January 8, 1992.

[10] DOE, Report of the Task Group on Operation of Department of Energy Tritium Facilities, DOE/EH-0198P, October 1991.

1963, the laboratory also released 6 million curies of radioactivity into the atmosphere.[11]

The Feed Materials Production Center near Cincinnati, Ohio, dumped thousands of tons of uranium waste at its site. The uranium waste leaked into nearby drinking wells which were used by nearby residents for two years until DOE finally notified them about the contamination. In settlement of a lawsuit brought by Ohio residents, DOE agreed to pay the residents $70 million dollars.[12]

WHISTLEBLOWERS

Unlike the commercial nuclear power plants and facilities in the United States, the nuclear weapons complex is largely free from outside regulation or oversight.[13] Radioactive materials under the control of DOE are exempted from a number of federal environmental laws like the Clean Water and Solid Waste Disposal Acts.[14] In effect, a veil of secrecy has surrounded the nuclear weapons complex and "whistleblowing" employees have played a critical role in revealing dangerous practices at the nuclear weapons production facilities.

DOE whistleblowers have exposed numerous abuses, including: the "loss" of 2.4 million pounds of mercury at the Oak Ridge facility in Tennessee; the discharge of over a half a million pounds of uranium at the Fernald Facility in Ohio; the exposure of an employee parking lot to high levels of radiation and the conversion of an abandoned, radioactive spent fuel reprocessing laboratory to a food storage warehouse at the Knolls Laboratory in New York; and the release of four million pounds

---

[11] See, Gray, p. 7.

[12] Reicher and Scherr, p. 36.

[13] 42 U.S.C. §2140(a). See, B. Finamore, *Regulating Hazardous and Mixed Waste at DOE Facilities: Reversing Decades of Environmental Neglect*, 9 Harvard Environmental Law Review, pp. 1, 83 (1984).

[14] See, 42 U.S.C. §6903(27); *Train v. Colorado P.I.R.G.*, 426 U.S. 1 (1976).

of carcinogenic, ozone-depleting carbon tetrachloride at a Colorado facility.[15]

DOE whistleblowers perform an important public service, but they are exposed to retaliation, harassment, and discrimination. Some have been subjected to long, isolated interrogations, forced to submit to polygraph tests, and ordered to see plant psychologists. They have been falsely accused of drug use or gambling and have been verbally and physically abused by fellow employees. Whistleblowers have faced reassignment to menial and often dangerous duties, loss of security clearance, denial of promotion, demotion, or termination.[16]

There has been wiretapping and illegal surveillance of suspected whistleblowers, including breakins and searches of their homes. In 1991, it was revealed that millions of dollars of surveillance equipment had been installed at several DOE facilities.[17] The Secretary of Energy, James Watkins, has since ordered the equipment confiscated.[18] The following are examples of whistleblowing.

Karen A. Pitts and Jacqueline M. Brever

In 1984, Karen A. Pitts and Jacqueline M. Brever started working as chemistry technicians at the Rocky Flats Facility in Colorado, the nation's only manufacturer of nuclear triggers for hydrogen bombs.[19] In October 1988, DOE temporarily shut down

---

[15] See, Slavin and Devine, *The Government's Secret War on Whistleblowers*, 18 ABA Barrister pp. 12, 15 (Spring 1991); Carpenter, "The Fight for Information," *Nuclear Times*, September 1986.

[16] See, Slavin & Devine; S. Kohn, *The Whistleblower Litigation Handbook: Environmental, Health, and Safety Claims* (1990).

[17] *Washington Post*, August 1, 1991, p. A1; Government Accountability Project, *Bridging the Gap*, (Fall, 1991).

[18] *New York Times*, August 2, 1991.

[19] *New York Times*, October 26, 1991.

the facility, just 18 miles north of Denver, because of numerous reports of safety and health violations including allegations that the plant was illegally incinerating radioactive wastes. In 1991, FBI agents investigated the alleged abuses, especially the reports of illegal waste incineration.[20]

Pitts and Brever were working at the time when DOE ordered the plant to be shut down and were sure that the plant was in fact incinerating radioactive wastes. Brever also kept a journal at work where she noted plant safety technicians sleeping on the job, playing cards, throwing radioactive rags at each other, and deliberately turning off radiation alarms in order to avoid having to respond to them. The journal also reported rooms that were deliberately or negligently contaminated and concrete floors that were so radioactive that moving across them was like "walking on sponges."[21]

The two women angered the plant's managers when they told them of their intent to cooperate with the FBI's investigation. Soon Pitts and Brever were being verbally harassed by managers and fellow employees and placed under constant surveillance at work and at home. Plant managers assigned the two women to perform potentially deadly tasks at work and intentionally exposed them to radiation in order to prevent them from talking to the FBI.[22] The women began to experience symptoms of radiation sickness including large bruises over their entire bodies. Pitts and Brever have filed civil lawsuits against the managers and have given the journals to the FBI in connection with a grand jury's criminal investigation of the plant.

Paula Nathaniel

In October 1988, Paula Nathaniel began working as a chemist for the Westinghouse Corporation at the Hanford Facility in Eastern Washington. Her duties included monitoring the dangerously unstable

---

[20] *Harper's Magazine*, February 1992.

[21] *Los Angeles Times*, November 10, 1991, p. A2.

[22] *Ibid.*

101-SY nuclear waste tank. Hydrogen gas builds up within the tank until it is expelled through the ventilation system. If the gas were to come in contact with a spark, a massive explosion could spread radioactive and toxic waste over hundreds of miles.

On October 24, 1990, Nathaniel reported a radiation protection technician lighting a cigarette near the waste tank. Nathaniel sent a report of the incident through the computer mail system. She was then promptly contacted by her supervisor who demanded that she withdraw her report because it would result in bad publicity if the press were to hear of the violation. When she refused, she first received a poor performance evaluation, and was then told by her supervisor to take a position elsewhere in the company.

Soon the harassment escalated. She began to receive late night phone calls at her home and at her parent's house and was often followed when not at work. Managers asked her fellow workers to remove files from her computer. In November 1990, she received an ultimatum from management. She was told that she could either take a minimum six-month leave of absence without pay, quit after writing a letter of resignation, or find a different position within the company.[23]

Inez Austin

In June 1990, Inez Austin, a senior engineer at Hanford Plant. was assigned to supervise the pumping of radioactive liquid waste from deteriorating underground tanks. Westinghouse officials were under considerable pressure to clean up the tanks quickly due to an agreement between DOE, the Environmental Protection Agency and the State of Washington. Austin refused when she discovered that some of the tanks contained ferrocyanide, a volatile chemical that could explode if the tanks were pumped dry.

When Austin refused to sign the reports stating that the pumping procedure was safe and on schedule, her supervisor placed a poor performance evaluation in her personnel file, then threatened to

---

[23] *Bridging the Gap*, p. 5.

fire her and suggested that she seek counseling. Austin was moved from her office to a hot, dusty trailer that aggravated her asthma. Westinghouse officials intercepted her mail for eight weeks and confiscated her office furniture, telephone, and computer.

Austin filed a complaint against the Westinghouse Corporation with the Department of Labor and agreed to a settlement of her charges of retaliation. In 1990, a DOE report confirmed Austin's finding that pumping the tanks could be potentially explosive and possibly cause a nuclear reaction. Since Austin spoke up, the pumping program has been delayed pending further analysis of the tanks.[24]

Charles D. Varnadore

In 1989, Varnadore, a technician at DOE's Oak Ridge National Laboratory in Tennessee, was treated for colon cancer. After returning to work, Varnadore began to complain to plant officials about health and safety problems[25] and later appeared on television expressing his concern about the elevated cancer rates among his fellow employees at the plant.

Executives of the subsidiary of the Martin-Marietta Company that operated Oak Ridge retaliated by isolating Varnadore from his fellow employees and then assigning him to perform mundane tasks in rooms containing radioactive waste, mercury, and asbestos. Varnadore filed a complaint with the Labor Department. The Labor Department ruled that the company had discriminated against Varnadore by putting him in a workplace of "questionable safety."[26]

---

[24] *The Progressive*, October 1991, pp. 15-20; *New York Times*, August 1, 1991, p. A18.

[25] *New York Times*, February 5, 1992, p. A16.

[26] *New York Times*, February 9, 1992.

INADEQUATE PROTECTION OF WHISTLEBLOWERS

The United States has many laws and procedures intended to protect whistleblowers.[27] For example, the Occupational Safety and Health Act protects employees who report safety violations that threaten physical harm or presents an imminent danger from employer retaliation.[28] There are also more specific laws that protect employees who report environmental violations.[29] In 1974, Congress passed the Energy Reorganization Act which protected whistleblowing employees who report health and safety violation at nuclear facilities.[30] However, the courts later held that these provisions apply only to employees of commercial nuclear power plants.[31]

Employees at DOE facilities must instead rely on DOE's internal regulations,[32] which provide less employee protection. The regulations do not protect employee disclosures to the media, public interest groups, states, or regulatory agencies like the Environmental Protection Agency and the Justice Department. They require the employee to certify that he exhausted all contractor employee protection procedures before bringing his complaint to the DOE and do not provide for Administrative Law Judges who have greater

---

[27] See, D. Westman, *Whistleblowing, the Law of Retaliatory Discharge* (1991).

[28] 29 U.S.C. §657(f)(1). See, Westman, pp. 72, 74.

[29] See, The Safe Water Drinking Act, 42 U.S.C. §300j-9(i); Clean Water Act, 33 U.S.C. §1367; Solid Waste Disposal Act, 42 U.S.C. §6971; Clean Air Act, 42 U.S.C. §7622.

[30] 42 U.S.C. §5851.

[31] See, *Adams v. Dole*, 927 F.2d 771 (4th Cir. 1991).

[32] *Criteria and Procedures for DOE Contractor Employee Protection Plan*, 10 CFR part 708, 57 Fed. Reg. 7533 (March 3, 1992).

independence and training than DOE Hearing Officers. The nuclear weapons facility employee also has no right to engage in discovery.[33]

The result is that, as recently stated by Representative Ron Wyden:

> "Congress has deliberately refused to protect DOE contractor employees who blow the whistle on horrendous environmental, safety, and health scandals."[34]

Representative Wyden has introduced legislation to amend the Energy Reorganization Act to explicitly protect contractor employees at DOE nuclear facilities.[35]

CONCLUSION

For years, the United States Government justified withholding information on its nuclear weapons facilities on national security grounds. DOE has abused this rationale to hide dangerous environment and health hazards. This problem has been exacerbated by government contractors who are supposed to operate the nuclear facilities for the public good, but are influenced by their desire to protect their own interests.

The end of the Cold War has begun to shift the United States from weapon production to weapon dismantlement and cleanup. Secretary of Energy Watkins has recently stated, "Nobody likes nuclear bombs. We want to get rid of the nuclear complex to the extent we

---

[33] See, Carpenter, *Analysis of New DOE Whistleblower Protection Rule*, (GAP Memorandum, March 6, 1992).

[34] Statement by Representative Ron Wyden, Whistleblower Protection Press Conference, Washington D.C., February 27, 1992.

[35] See, H.R. 776, 102d. Cong., 1st. Sess. (1992).

can."[36] Watkins has outlined an extensive plan for plant closures and a far greater commitment of money and personnel to environmental cleanup. These changes also call for less secrecy and greater openness and public accountability, including more protection for whistleblowers.

---

[36] *Los Angeles Times*, December 17, 1991.

Human Rights Watch

Human Rights Watch, which monitors and promotes observance of internationally recognized human rights worldwide, is composed of Africa Watch, Americas Watch, Asia Watch, Helsinki Watch, Middle East Watch, and the Fund for Free Expression.

Addresses for Human Rights Watch

485 Fifth Avenue
New York, NY 10017
Tel: (212) 972-8400
Fax: (212) 972-0905

1522 K Street, NW #910
Washington, DC 20005
Tel: (202) 371-6592
Fax: (202) 371-0124

10951 West Pico Boulevard #203
Los Angeles, CA 90064
Tel: (213) 475-3070
Fax: (213) 475-5613

90 Borough High Street
London UK SE1 1LL
Tel: (071) 378-8008
Fax: (071) 378-8029

Natural Resources Defense Council

The Natural Resources Defense Council is a nonprofit membership organization dedicated to protecting the planet's natural resources and to improving the quality of the human environment. With 170,000 members and a staff of lawyers, scientists, and environmental specialists, NRDC combines the power of law, the power of science, and the power of people in defense of the environment. NRDC develops and advocates effective solutions to a wide range of pressing international problems, including global warming, nuclear proliferation, energy, trade, deforestation, and international environmental rights and institutions.

Addresses for the Natural Resources Defense Council

40 W. 20th Street
New York, NY 10011
(212) 727-2700

1350 New York Avenue, N.W.
Washington, DC 20005
(202) 783-7800

71 Stevenson
San Francisco, CA 94105
(415) 777-0220

617 South Olive Street
Los Angeles, CA 90014
(213) 892-1500

212 Merchant Street
Honolulu, HI 96813
(808) 533-1075